FULL
OF
BULL

FINANCIAL TIMES

In an increasingly competitive world, it is quality
of thinking that gives an edge—an idea that opens new
doors, a technique that solves a problem, or an insight
that simply helps make sense of it all.

We work with leading authors in the various arenas
of business and finance to bring cutting-edge thinking
and best-learning practices to a global market.

It is our goal to create world-class print publications
and electronic products that give readers
knowledge and understanding that can then be
applied, whether studying or at work.

To find out more about our business
products, you can visit us at www.ftpress.com.

FULL
OF
BULL

Do What Wall Street Does, Not What it Says,
To Make Money in the Market

Stephen T. McClellan

Vice President, Publisher: Tim Moore
Associate Publisher and Director of Marketing: Amy Neidlinger
Executive Editor: Jim Boyd
Editorial Assistant: Pamela Boland
Development Editor: Russ Hall
Digital Marketing Manager: Julie Phifer
Publicist: Amy Fandrei
Marketing Coordinator: Megan Colvin
Cover Designer: Ingredient
Managing Editor: Gina Kanouse
Project Editor: Chelsey Marti
Copy Editor: Water Crest Publishing, Inc.
Proofreader: Harrison Ridge Editorial Services
Indexer: Erika Millen
Senior Compositor: Gloria Schurick
Manufacturing Buyer: Dan Uhrig

This book is sold with the understanding that neither the author nor the publisher is engaged in rendering legal, accounting or other professional services or advice by publishing this book. Each individual situation is unique. Thus, if legal or financial advice or other expert assistance is required in a specific situation, the services of a competent professional should be sought to ensure that the situation has been evaluated carefully and appropriately. The author and the publisher disclaim any liability, loss or risk resulting, directly or indirectly, from the use or application of any of the contents of this book.

FT Press offers excellent discounts on this book when ordered in quantity for bulk purchases or special sales. For more information, please contact U.S. Corporate and Government Sales, 1-800-382-3419, corpsales@pearsontechgroup.com. For sales outside the U.S., please contact International Sales at international@pearsoned.com.

Company and product names mentioned herein are the trademarks or registered trademarks of their respective owners.

Printed in the United States of America

First Printing October 2007

ISBN-10: 0-13-236011-X
ISBN-13: 978-0-13-2360111

Pearson Education LTD.
Pearson Education Australia PTY, Limited.
Pearson Education Singapore, Pte. Ltd.
Pearson Education North Asia, Ltd.
Pearson Education Canada, Ltd.
Pearson Educatión de Mexico, S.A. de C.V.
Pearson Education—Japan
Pearson Education Malaysia, Pte. Ltd.

Library of Congress Cataloging-in-Publication Data

McClellan, Stephen T.
  Full of bull : do what Wall Street does, not what it says, to make money in the market / Stephen T. McClellan.
    p. cm.
  ISBN 0-13-236011-X (hardback : alk. paper) 1. Stocks—United States. 2. Investments—United States. 3. Investment analysis—United States. 4. Wall Street (New York, N.Y.) I. Title.
  HG4910.M3696 2008
  332.63'220973—dc22

                          2007022483

To Elizabeth,
my love, my bride, my friend

Contents

Acknowledgments

This book was materially enhanced by input from a few trusted Wall Street veterans whom I have known for most of my career. They reviewed the manuscript and made several worthy suggestions. My old friend Peter Anastos spent his career in the mutual fund industry, the last several years before retirement as head portfolio manager of the Alliance Capital technology fund. Jim Lee was an institutional salesman at the small firm where I started in 1971, has been an investment manager over the years, and is an astute observer of the Street as well as investment trends. Over the decades, he has seen it all, from the buyside perspective. George McDougall, a friend since first grade, was instrumental in determining the title and aided in the editing. John Korvin, a golf partner who skins me regularly, and Mike Walsh, a comrade involved in technology market research, gave me valuable suggestions. Jim Boyd at Prentice Hall guided the publication process. The Barbara Hendra Agency assisted in marketing promotion. I appreciate their constructive counsel.

The foremost person assisting in the preparation of this book was Joyce Padua. She works with me as my personal assistant. We slogged each morning for a few hours, me buried under copious notes on one side of my desk, she sitting across in front of the computer. She did her share of editing, too. Now she thinks she's an expert investor. Another valuable contributor was my freelance editor Michael Denneny in New York, who brought order and clarity to my jumbled prose.

Then there is my progeny. Laurel Almerinda remembers the labors of my first book. As an artsy, creative, and driven USC graduate film school alum, she's pursuing a career as a writer and director in Los Angeles. Justin McClellan toiled for his engineering degree at Boston University and is now employed in the aerospace field while eagerly mastering the investment ropes of managing his own portfolio of stocks. They constantly offer unsolicited parental advice to keep me in line.

Finally, my bride Elizabeth Barlow, a painter who spent her career in the arts, the opera, and ballet, became the love of my life as this book was in midstream. Her feline, Figaro, came along with her and promptly took over as master of the house. Several times Elizabeth overheard me casually giving practical and what I thought was obvious investment advice to someone. It was intuitive to me as a professional insider, but an enlightening observation to outsiders. She usually reacted by inquiring if I had addressed that in my book. Amazingly, in many cases, I hadn't. So I immediately jotted the suggestion into the book. Elizabeth was instrumental in helping me visualize investing from the eyes of a non-professional outsider.

About the Author

Stephen McClellan was a Wall Street investment analyst for 32 years, covering high-tech stocks as a supervisory analyst. He was a First Vice President at Merrill Lynch for 18 years, and ranked on the annual Institutional Investor All-American Research Team 19 consecutive times, the *Wall Street Journal* Poll for 7 years, and is in the *Journal's* Hall of Fame. He was a Vice President at Salomon Brothers for 8 years, before that in a similar position at Spencer Trask, and was the industry analyst with the U.S. Department of Commerce before commencing his Wall Street career.

Mr. McClellan is a Chartered Financial Analyst (CFA), a member of the New York Society of Security Analysts and the CFA Institute, was President of the New York Computer Industry Analyst Group, and President and Founder of the Software/Services Analyst Group. He has made television appearances on CBS, CNN *MoneyLine*, CNBC, and *Wall Street Week*, and given presentations to numerous organizations, conferences, and to companies such as IBM, Apple, Automatic Data Processing, and Electronic Data Systems. Mr. McClellan has published articles in the *London Financial Times*, *New York Times*, *Forbes*, and others. His MBA in Finance is from George Washington University.

Preface

This book is for the individual investor. It is all about investing, not trading, because investing is the way to make money in the stock market. Transaction-oriented Wall Street, unfortunately, tends to discourage and even hinder proper investing. Brokerage advice can be misleading, even contradictory. Professional insiders know better than to take the Street literally. You need to take the same approach. Do what Wall Street does, not what it says. This book will show you how to avoid Street pitfalls, circumvent inappropriate research guidance, correctly interpret Wall Street commentary and opinions, properly assess statements by corporate executives, and put news media reports in their proper context. It will provide you with an understanding of the confusing and conflicted ways of Wall Street, so you can maneuver around these influences and make more profitable long-term investment decisions.

Life sometimes shifts in unforeseen directions. For 32 years, I was so consumed by my job as a securities analyst on Wall Street that my natural inclination was just to continue grinding away for a couple more years before hanging it up. I had no compelling new venture or life plan that I was anxious to embark on. But as the stock market bubble deflated in 2000 and 2001, the economics of brokerage firm research were permanently altered. The discrediting of analysts, elimination of investment-bank research subsidies, and shrinkage in commission fees ushered in an era of parsimonious research budgets. Senior analysts could no longer be paid the vast sums of the past. At the Four Seasons Resort on Hawaii's Kona coast, as I sat by the pool after my fifth Mai Tai, it hit me. I could add a couple more years of adventure to my life if I opted out. So the timing all coincided—in early 2003, I tossed in the towel and concluded a long career as an analyst.

On my first day of retirement, when depression might have ensued from the vast new void in my life, I headed off to Utah to ski with my son and attend the screening of my daughter's new short-subject movie at the Sundance Film Festival. This marked the first time in over three decades that I boarded a plane without bringing along a carry-on bag full of work. I was savoring the prospect of perusing the newspapers and maybe reading a history book, when a guy in a suit plopped down next to me and inquired as to my business. Upon learning that I had stock market expertise, he began firing off a series of simplistic investment questions. After more than three decades of analyzing, researching, writing on, and talking about stocks, the last thing I felt like doing on my first trip free of Wall Street was to chat about investing—especially to educate a naive, nettlesome passenger who was probing me for silver bullets. I quickly wriggled out of the conversation. Then a jarring realization hit me— there was a whole world of individual investors out there, struggling to make money in the stock market with little knowledge of how the Wall Street investment game is really played.

Over the following two or three years, I filled up a notebook with observations and insights that might be useful to an individual investor. My previous book in the early 1980s, *The Coming Computer Industry Shakeout*, concluded with a brief chapter on basic principles for individual investors. Although rudimentary, it made a splash with readers and the press. This time, with *Full of Bull*, the entire book is devoted to such investment maxims. My style is opinionated, forthright, and direct. My views may be controversial, but I try to emulate the revered sportscaster Howard Cossell and "tell it like it is." These are my own conclusions—insight acquired during decades of working on Wall Street.

I grew up in Wilmette, Illinois, ran track at New Trier High School, and tooled around in a jeep delivering newspapers each summer. My initial intrigue with the stock market and Wall Street surfaced during college, so I buttressed my liberal arts economics major at Syracuse University by taking additional business and finance courses. When I heard that a two-person stock brokerage firm in Chicago might be in need of summer help, I leaped. Morton D. Cahn was an octogenarian and the most senior member of the Midwest Stock Exchange. His halcyon days had been the 1920s, but in the 1960s, he still kept a tiny one-room office going and spent his days on the exchange floor doing maybe a dozen trades a day. All summer in that office, I devoured every facet of the business—calculated commissions, messenger-ed securities around the city, took transaction orders over the phone, studied a text on bonds during my downtime, and handled the office all alone when the old line office manager was away on vacation. By Labor Day, I knew my career would be on Wall Street.

Some of the paychecks I collected from that stint were destined for investment. I was gung-ho to become an honest-to-goodness stockholder myself. My dictatorial father, who was springing for my college expenses, vetoed the idea. But I was adamant and put in a buy order for five shares of Union Carbide at $91. When I divulged my "shareholder" status to him, he was furious and I was unyielding. I guess I was coming of age and beginning to stand up for myself. Everyday during my senior year at Syracuse, on shirt cardboards, I recorded Union Carbide's opening, high, low, and closing prices and its trading volume. I cared. You can't imagine the satisfaction I felt every three months when I received my dividend check for $6.25. And the next summer, I sold the shares for over $109—my maiden investment had produced an inspiring capital gain!

In those college days, New York City was our venue during Thanksgiving vacations. Amidst jazz clubs, hockey games, and other cavorting, I spent Friday (the market being open) wandering around Wall Street as an anxious outsider wanting to become an insider: at the New York Stock Exchange, the American Exchange, Trinity Church, the streets, bookstores, and even brokerage lobbies. My buddies were dumbfounded that I would waste a day of our precious, exciting school break in Gotham trolling the canyons of Wall Street. For me, though, it was Priority Number One.

In the Navy, as an operations officer aboard a ship based in Norfolk, I devoured *The Wall Street Journal* when in port, scrutinized *Forbes* magazine while on watch, compiled a notebook of research, and planned my strategy to reach Wall Street. I had a meager few-hundred dollars invested in one or two stocks. Shortly before mustering out of the military, while preliminarily knocking on Wall Street doors, I received some emphatic counsel from a Merrill Lynch personnel-department interviewer. I needed a Master's degree in Business Administration if I hoped to advance very far in the business, he told me (as if I could run across the street, grab a graduate degree, and be back that afternoon!). It was daunting to ponder the prospect of three more years in school before reaching the Street.

So, during the late 1960s as the Vietnam War raged, I donned my uniform, interviewed, and was rubberstamped at George Washington University Business School, where my dad had earned his law degree in 1929. Upon settling in Washington, D.C., I landed a day job with the U.S. Department of Commerce. There, I assisted the office equipment industry analyst, Jim Carr, a senior veteran who called me his amanuensis. Jim showed me the basics of how to write. I was immersed in tracking and publishing reports on the rising computer industry. Three years later, MBA in hand, I blanketed Street broker-age firms seeking interviews. With no clue as to what specialty I pre-ferred—institutional sales, trading, investment banking, or research—I haphazardly tossed around glossy rèsumès. One bou-tique firm, Spencer Trask, noted my computer industry expertise and bumped me up to the research director, whose offer was the only one forthcoming. I took it instantly, starting at an $18,000 annual salary. The MBA turned out to be irrelevant; familiarity with the data-pro-cessing field was the trigger. Life is strange.

That debut day in 1971 was eons removed from my walk-off in 2003. My first six years on Wall Street were a steep learning experi-ence at Spencer Trask, a small, respected, research-focused broker-age. I was mentored by the electronics analyst who hired me, Otis Bradley; became a full-fledged analyst myself; and enjoyed a coddled existence at this old-school, genteel, white-shoe firm. Six years later, in 1977, I made a leap to Salomon Brothers, an aggressive, trading-oriented, highly profitable firm endowed with stellar professionals and a recognized, confident èlan. It was a cauldron, but it introduced me to the changing real world of Wall Street. After eight years, I slid over to Merrill Lynch and stayed there for 18 years. Merrill was becoming a heavyweight in research, a household word and leader on Wall Street, and a good place to be as an analyst. At Merrill I achieved #1 status in *Institutional Investor* magazine's analyst rankings for sev-eral years, moved to San Francisco, and operated from there for the remainder of my career.

A couple of years ago, a casual investor mentioned at lunch, before a round of golf at our club, that he was about to purchase a particular stock in the aerospace-defense sector. His justification was something like "nine Wall Street Buy recommendations and only one

Hold, all the favorable Street opinions have been in place for a year or longer, and the consensus price objective is some $18 above the current level." He obviously believed all this Street talk, having no idea that, given precisely the situation he described, perhaps he ought to be <u>avoiding</u> the stock.

In contrast, as a Street professional, my interpretation was that the one lonely Hold stance was really a Sell indication (probably insightful and timely), and should be given more credence. Street analysts use the terms Hold or Neutral to subtly indicate a negative view, avoiding the word Sell in order to preclude adverse reaction from company management and major institutional owners of the stock. I also thought all the Buy opinions were likely growing stale, so there might be more downgrades ahead shortly. My golfing partner was late to the party and had undoubtedly missed the big gains in the stock. Further, I assumed those analyst price targets probably had been boosted a couple of times already to justify the continued Buy ratings—and insiders know that such price targets are nothing more than wild guesses anyway, concocted to help hype the stock. My skeptical assessment would be shared by almost anyone on Wall Street, but my golf bud, being a typical individual investor, misinterpreted the situation. From all my years on Wall Street, I understand that a key to superior investing is decoding the Street's confusing (if not misleading) doubletalk and ignoring or sometimes even defying its advice. Nevertheless, most investors fall right in line like true believers.

My golfing friend and I, when it came to investments, did not speak the same language. Wall Street directs its efforts and advice to the managers of big mutual fund portfolios and hedge funds. Similar to a baseball manager talking to his players or other league officials, the Street assumes that other professionals in the business understand the nuanced manner in which the game is played; assumes they are able to use research material appropriately (i.e., not take it literally); and expects them to react in a certain manner. But when it comes to the individual investor, there is a massive disconnect. What is needed is plain speaking, by a Wall Street veteran such as me, to unscramble the confounding practices of the Street in terms a layperson can comprehend.

The individual investor is often misled by Wall Street's ambiguous ways. What investors are missing is the knowledge necessary to deal with the Street; how to put the deluge of stock information in the proper perspective and make their own investment decisions. It's not enough to tap into the Internet, tune into CNBC, scan the financial section of the newspaper, devour magazines like *Money*, listen to a broker, or even read the typical book on how to invest. Keeping in touch with all these sources helps, but the information must still be utilized effectively. The misleading actions of Wall Street must be taken into account. What should you make of a Street recommendation upgrade from Sell to Hold or Neutral? If a stock is downgraded from Buy to Neutral, should you hold it or sell it? After a stock price target is reached, the target is raised and the investor is told to continue buying. Wasn't the initial target real? And if so, shouldn't the investor be told to Sell once the objective is achieved? You get the picture. You just don't have a chance unless you decipher all the confusing, unpredictable, and often counterproductive Wall Street babble.

The purpose of this book is to expose the puzzling, deceptive, conflicted behavior of Wall Street that so disadvantages individual investors, tripping them up in their attempts to invest properly and rationally. The output from securities analysts is highly useful as background research. Analysts are steeped in company and industry expertise, provide helpful commentary in reaction to events and news, and publish handy earnings estimates. But an investor needs to know what to discount and how to put Street research in perspective—how to separate the wheat from the chaff. An individual investor must grasp how the system works and be able to factor this aspect into his or her investment approach. Once armed with an insider's understanding of all the Street's subtleties, you can be your own investment analyst. My strategies will equip you to evaluate companies, select stocks, and take advantage of your position, free from the many constraints that inhibit professionals.

Stephen T. McClellan

September, 2007

1

Decoding Wall Street's Well-Kept Secrets

As a securities analyst for 32 years, I am amazed that naive investors can be so misled by Wall Street doubletalk. You can be an astute investor only if you fathom the puzzling and often deceptive nature of the Street. Do what Wall Street does, not what it says. Don't take the Street literally. Wall Street operates in strange, ambiguous ways that it would prefer to keep secret. Its research cannot be trusted. The individual investor is an afterthought, mostly neglected by analysts and brokerage research departments. Analysts' opinions change and their statements move stocks. The media passes along analyst commentary and prints their views. Corporate executives react to Street sentiment, and attempt to influence their stock prices. Wall Street cannot be ignored. By decoding the confusing, cryptic Wall Street practices, you can unlock the handcuffs that inhibit superior investing. If you understand the research game to the same degree that professional portfolio managers do, the playing field will be more even.

In mid-1985, I decided to take a new job on Wall Street and make a shift to Merrill Lynch, but I had to sit tight for 10 days. I was scheduled as Louis Rukeyser's guest under the Salomon Brothers moniker and couldn't resign gracefully until off the set of *Wall Street Week*. I

already felt edgy on arrival in the remote horse country of Owings
Mills, Maryland. After cooling my heels a couple hours in the studio,
Lou, who hadn't finished writing his commentary, wasn't ready to
tape the show at the normal time that Friday evening, an hour before
it aired on PBS. So my appearance was one of his infrequent programs that went on live—adding pressure and more time to stew.
Seated just off the set for the first half of the program with a pitcher
of water, I was told to be still or the viewers might see the movement
of my shadow. Nervously, I consumed most of the jug and badly
needed relief about the time the hostess grabbed my arm to strut me
out to the couch in front of the cameras and panelists. My bladder
bulged as the hostess whispered to me and we wheeled into camera
view, "Don't trip on the platform, three million viewers are watching."
I sank down into the gigantic soft sofa, feeling like a midget looking
up at Rukeyser, who towered over me in his high-perched chair. All
my hours of practiced answers flew out of my head. I was babbling. It
was like truth serum, but I survived. Analysts like me are not accustomed to being grilled. We normally have the upper hand. At least
we're good at faking aplomb and we rarely come unraveled. This
book puts you in Rukeyser's shoes. It's intended to unravel Wall
Street security analysts and their research.

What is a Wall Street Securities Analyst?

To comprehend Street research, you must first be familiar with the
function of a securities analyst. I am talking about an analyst at a brokerage firm investment bank, not an in-house stock analyst at mutual
funds, banks, or investment management firms that cater only to the
portfolio managers within their own firm. The job function of brokerage analysts is to conduct research on companies and industries and
"sell" it to the brokerage institutional clients and secondarily to individual investors. A typical Street analyst heads a small team of associates, is situated in New York (I was in New York for 20 years and then
relocated to San Francisco for the last twelve years of my career), has
maybe a dozen years experience, and is in the 30 to 40 age range. The
ideal analyst has an MBA degree, should be a Chartered Financial
Analyst (CFA), is adept at reading and interpreting financial statements, understanding and building complicated mathematical

earnings models on a computer, writing research reports, talking and interviewing, and selling/marketing. This is a wish list, as rarely do analysts have all these qualifications.

The primary requisite of any analyst is to be an expert on a particular industry sector and group of companies therein. There are analysts covering areas such as high-tech semiconductors or software, retail specialty stores, the oil and gas industry, biotech, airlines, utilities, and banks. I began covering the entire computer industry in the 1970s when it was small, gravitated to focusing on software and computer services in the 1980s, and then covered only computer services starting in the 1990s (companies like EDS, Automatic Data Processing, and Accenture). Analysts conduct research on and rigorously track a limited number of companies in their chosen industry area. They must understand the dynamics, influences, and underpinnings of the industry, and be exceptionally familiar with as much detail on each company as possible—elements like the financials, products, competitive position, management, strategies, and research and development. Analysts must have an ability to judge executives, assess the impact or effect of any number of influences on a company, have the vision to see the big picture amidst tumultuous current pressures on a stock, and analyze a company's outlook with incomplete information in an unclear situation.

It is common for analysts to have worked in the industry they are covering before starting on Wall Street. Analyst industry expertise is more important than a background in securities, investment or finance. I became savvy on the computer industry while employed at the U.S. Department of Commerce tracking the sector there. Wall Street recognized my knowledge of that area and hired me for that reason, not because of my MBA degree.

The next analyst qualification is an understanding of the stock market, investment, and securities (stocks, bonds, options, convertibles, etc.). This is basic stuff, things like listed vs. NASDAQ-traded securities, bid and ask spreads, stock buybacks, dividends, share issuances, stock options, debt (bonds), and all the mechanical aspects of the stock market. Sometimes this is obtained while earning an MBA degree or on the job, in the business, as a junior start-up analyst; and it is enhanced in the process of acquiring the professional CFA designation. I did both, but was further ahead of the game due to my college summer job at a small brokerage firm in Chicago, reading financial newspapers/magazines and books, investing on my own, and following the market for years before I landed on Wall Street.

Street analysts also need to have some grasp on the economy. My undergraduate degree was in economics. Several economic factors impact stocks and company fundamentals. Analysts should be conversant with elements like interest rates, employment, GDP, inflation, recessions, government spending and borrowing, foreign currencies, and international trade. An MBA degree is a key source to absorb background in economic disciplines.

The securities analyst's role is to determine the industry and individual company outlook in the sector covered, conclude whether the stocks are attractive investments (a Buy opinion) or likely to perform poorly (a Sell), write up these findings in research reports, and monitor all this on a continuing basis. A key mission is to then verbally communicate this research to the brokerage firm's institutional investor clients, and other key audiences like the in-house sales force and traders, and the outside media. Analysts on Wall Street must sell their research, that is, market their product and views. Notice I left out retail individual investors. Analysts don't deal with them directly. To be proficient at this so-called marketing, analysts must be outgoing. No shy types. They make presentations to single portfolio managers or a room full of institutional investors. Analysts have to be convincing on the telephone or over their firm's squawk box. They must have conviction, be strong, opinionated, confident, and come across as cool, intelligent, and balanced, like a 747 airline pilot during a turbulent thunderstorm (my worst nightmare). This requires personality, character, charm, and the need to be colorful and engaging. (Of course, I was all that and more—did I mention humility?)

The brokerage institutional salespeople caters directly to the portfolio managers, traders, and analysts at the firm's institutional clients—mutual funds, hedge funds, pension funds, banks, and other financial institutions. They constantly, all day long, carry the analyst's research message to these institutions, in person, on the phone, or by email. Salesmen may cover a half dozen such institutions and talk with perhaps five or ten key contacts at each one. They also help sell to these big clients initial public offerings (IPOs) and secondary share issuances their firms are underwriting, and set up meetings between their analysts or corporate executives and these institutional customers. Traders execute sizeable buy and sell orders on behalf of major clients and attempt to make money for the brokerage firm's own account by trading stocks. Investment bankers deal with corporations, governments, and other entities in need of such financial services as selling stock or bonds, doing mergers and acquisitions, and structuring complicated financial/investment transactions.

What's a typical day in the life of an analyst? During the latter portion of my career I was located in San Francisco, where the stock market opens at 6:30 AM, so my hours were on the early side. My firm's morning conference call, where research analysts present pertinent new views or updates, commenced at 4:15 AM. I rolled out of bed at 4:10 AM, tossed on my sweats, and jumped on the horn. As this live broadcast was to hundreds of offices worldwide, it was critical to not fall asleep or screw up. Then, after donning slacks and a sweater, I drove through dark streets, grabbed a giant coffee, cream and sugar, and was at my desk by 6 AM. Things were now happening full blast as it was 9 AM in New York. The sales force was on my case to call key institutional clients to add color to the comments I made on the earlier morning call. My stock screen was racing with price changes, news stories, and other information in my face. Emails by the dozens pleaded for responses, opinions, scheduling, and all sorts of other matters. My team was in the office, wanting to chat or discuss research. No help from my administrative assistant, who waltzed in at about 7:30 AM, and worked fairly normal hours. At some point, I hustled a couple blocks over to a local hotel for a breakfast meeting with a mutual fund portfolio manager.

Back in the office around 9. *The Wall Street Journal* called. An executive from a company I covered was in town and showed up at my door mid-morning. We discussed his firm's business outlook for an hour. My 16-ounce takeout coffee got cold, but I was still sipping it. I had to scrutinize, in advance, a detailed computer earnings model of a company that would report its results at 1 PM this particular day, after the market closed. Soup at my desk for lunch, the first thing I'd eaten all day. The earnings results hit the tape. We did instant analysis, prepared questions, and tuned in on the company's 2 PM investor conference call. It was over at 3, and after a few minutes of pondering and quick analysis, I ground out a research report. Maybe about 5:30 I waved goodbye to the garage attendants, who gave me no credit since I didn't top a 12-hour day. Alongside me in the front car seat was a portfolio of material to review during the evening with a bowl of ice cream and the baseball game quietly on TV in the background.

Abnormal events in the day of an analyst are normal. I was summoned to a payphone while atop the High Sierras in Yosemite by H. Ross Perot (the other campers were impressed) and was detained by passport control officers at an Italian border crossing the night Aldo Moro was assassinated. I have broadcast my research comments over the squawk box system from aircraft carriers and jumped on the box from phone booths in Vienna cafes. Sometimes I took advantage of the firm's Chicago Cubs Wrigley Field courtesy suite up behind home plate, squeezing in an occasional night game where I had misspent the bulk of my youth in the bleachers. I've witnessed Michael Jordan in the NBA playoffs, gate crashed the Cannes Film Festival, bumped into Queen Elizabeth exiting a London theatre, sipped cocktails at Raffles bar in Singapore, and basked on Waikiki Beach. But there are dodgy scenarios too. Our Kansas City car service driver that I had used for years on client visits there turned up as a fugitive when the police found multiple homicide victims in his home. This mild mannered chauffeur was on the phone with our Chicago sales desk apologizing that he wasn't available for the next assignment, while law enforcement was in pursuit. He was later apprehended, convicted, and given five life sentences.

And then there was September 11th. Jenny Dugan, a junior analyst on my team and I were in New York to conduct a day of one-on-one meetings with investors. Two clients had requested the 8 AM lower Manhattan area time slot, Fred Alger Management and another bigger mutual fund, which ended up getting the nod. Jenny was meeting with the latter client in the World Trade Center tower at 8:50 AM, while I was uptown. The first plane hit one floor below the Fred Alger offices where our meeting would have been were it not for that other request. Tragically, no one at that firm survived. All of us in the business were deeply saddened by the events of that day as we all knew people who lost their lives. Jenny and her group found the stairwell overcrowded and exited via the elevator. To this day she is reticent to discuss it and has hidden away her WTC-2 security building pass issued that morning revealing her photograph and the September 11th date.

The greatest reward a securities analyst can obtain is being brilliantly correct on a major investment recommendation. I discovered Fiserv as an emerging stock early in the late 1980s, constantly pounded the table with a resounding Buy, and watched it rise steadily in price for more than a decade. A more established company, Computer Sciences, had been a lackluster performer for years when its prospects gradually started to improve. I was the earliest analyst on the Street to recognize the metamorphosis and my favorable opinion shift proved to be an insightful call. It was a winner for years. Conversely, the worst nightmare for an analyst is having a recommendation go wrong. All analysts vividly remember their bad picks.

The perks of an analyst's job aren't bad either. The best place on earth for golf is Augusta National in Georgia, the site of the Masters tournament. Even for Tiger Woods or Jack Nicklaus, that place is sacred. The ghosts of legends like Bobby Jones and Ben Hogan loom down the fairways. So you might imagine the awe that Augusta inspires in a mediocre duffer like myself. When the chairman of an Atlanta-based software firm, John Imlay, part owner of the Falcons NFL football team, inquired of my availability to take in a game from the owner's box, loiter in the locker room, and chat with the coach on the field, I could barely get the yes word out of my stammering lips. And while that was rolling off my tongue, he mentioned as an aside that we'd also be motoring to Augusta afterwards for a couple days of golf there.

Magnolia Drive, the Butler cabin, dining in the clubhouse, each of the 18 holes that I was so familiar with from TV coverage—the entire venue was a dreamy, mystical ecstasy. Caddies handed us the golf club we were supposed to use, not the one we could hit best given our ability—normal people can't hit a two-iron. I maxed out my credit card in the golf shop, was told "those green jackets on that rack are for members only," swiped all the logo-ed stationery out of my room, and feigned a nonchalant demeanor the whole time. My game was atrocious. What do you expect playing on hallowed ground as if in the presence of Divinity? Well, you can see the outing was a highlight in my life, and it wasn't a bad locale to chat up management.

The most trying aspect for security analysts on Wall Street is the insecure feeling of always being vulnerable to anything that might impact the stocks they cover. The fear stems from realizing that at anytime during a business day a company under coverage might announce dramatic surprising news. An analyst in this circumstance must scramble, jump on a conference call, respond to an avalanche of inquiries from the sales force and investors, and instantly assess the situation to form an accurate view. This is difficult enough if the analyst is in the office with all necessary resources at hand. It's a disaster if it happens during a tightly packed all-day client meeting trip, while on an airline flight, vacationing on a cruise ship, or on the golf course. Analysts can never relax on days the stock market is open. Even on holiday in August we monitor our Blackberries and call in periodically every business day, just like a doctor on call.

Heavy travel is inherent in the investment analyst profession. Travel stories are legend. Seated in the last row on a flight from Seattle, I could see before take-off that the emergency exit door behind me was left ajar. Daylight was peering through the opening. Upon pointedly notifying the attendant, she phoned the flight deck but, without inspecting it, the pilots pronounced the hatch secure from the cockpit because there was no indicator light on. My seatbelt was strapped on like a tourniquet. I knew the outcome—we wouldn't be airborne long without pressurization—and was flabbergasted by the crew's attitude. One circle of the airport, and we were landing again. Bulky maintenance brutes tried slamming the hatch to force it tight. They were still banging away when I grabbed my carry-on baggage and bailed, my confidence shot. Several others followed. So much for aircraft structural integrity.

Twice I've been on a plane that was struck by lightning, a bright flash outside the window and a thunderous boom. Good for the nerves. I knew a fellow analyst at a different firm who was on the Pan Am 103 Lockerbie flight, blown out of the air by a terrorist bomb. Several of us attended the funeral. A little macabre, but with such extensive travel, analysts are exposed to risks. An associate's flight from New York to San Francisco hit sudden turbulence, plummeted 10,000 feet, the service cart and attendants hit the ceiling, red was splattered all over the floor thought to be blood but later found to be red wine, and the plane made an emergency landing in Kansas City.

After realizing the function and role of Wall Street investment analysts, you need the rest of the story. That's what this book is all about—the reality and well-kept secrets of Street research. To be effective, investors need to comprehend how Wall Street operates, to work around it in some cases, and to take advantage of it in other situations. You will be able to invest on a par with the professionals once the strange, deceptive ways of Wall Street are demystified.

Wall Street Analysts Are Bad at Stock Picking

It's a shocking truth, but the way the system is oriented, stock picking is not the analyst's job. Until recently, brokerage firms did not even track the accuracy of their analyst opinions. The skill was neglected for a long time. It was just not an important part of the analyst job description. Wall Street analysts are supposed to pursue information about the companies and industries they cover, evaluate and gain insight on the future prospect of those companies, assess their investment value, and form opinions on the outlook for their stocks. We are required to assign investment ratings such as "Buy" or "Sell" to indicate a net overall evaluation. And that's where the real issues start to surface. Professional qualifications, incentive compensation, and the main audience—*institutional* investors—do not stress this function of stock picking at all. An *Institutional Investor* magazine survey in the fall of 2006 asked the buyside institutions—mutual funds, banks, pension funds, and hedge funds that buy and sell stocks through the brokerage firms—to indicate the most important attributes they sought in sellside (brokerage) Street analysts. Of 12 factors ranked in order of priority, stock selection placed 11th. Obviously, this skill is not an analyst job function required by their foremost audience. As a result, stock picking is neglected.

For years, the *Wall Street Journal* published a quarterly dartboard contest. The expert stock selections by analysts and portfolio managers did no better than those picked randomly. In another test, a website featuring a newsletter called the "Paradox Investor" assessed the performance of all Sell- and Hold-rated stocks on the Street for a two-year period ending in the fall of 2003. This portfolio of negatively viewed stocks gained 53.5%, more than 75 percentage points better than the market. When stocks have several Sell recommendations, there is nowhere else for that stock to go but up. Once the fourth or fifth Sell opinion is issued on a stock, it is probably ready to recover. Analysts are usually late and are also copycats. Mutual fund money managers are no great shakes either. Barron's conducts a poll every six months. In spring 2006, the professionals' Sell recommendations from the year before had surged ahead by 28% compared to their Buys that climbed just 13%. And in spring 2007, these pros' picks from the prior year actually dropped 2% but their pans were up 6%. Daunting.

If that's not enough proof, Charles Schwab rates stocks A to F. From May 2002 through Oct. 2003, its F-rated names, those deemed to have the poorest prospects, performed the best of any category, ahead 30%. In another survey, the *Wall Street Journal* reported that Investars.com ranked Street research firms by how each one's stock picks performed compared to the S&P 500 over a one-year span ending in May of 2005. You've probably never heard of four of the top five: Weiss Ratings, Columbine Capital, Ford Equity Research, and Channel Trend. The major brokerage Buy-rated stock results were strewn further down the list. Pretty much the same pattern held true when evaluated over a four-year term. The Street pushes analysts to emphasize institutional handholding and marketing, not research and stock recommendations. No wonder the record stinks.

Insightful research analysis has little bearing on the accuracy of Buy or Sell recommendations. Brokerage analysts are usually good at providing thorough, informative company and industry research. But their investment rating track record is mediocre, and in many cases inverse to their compensation. The system spawns this fatal flaw because analysts are being compensated mainly for profile, status, clout, and industry/company knowledge rather than for investment opinion accuracy. The extreme influence and impact of analysts can result in great damage when investors are misled. Jack Grubman is the poster boy example here. As a telecommunications analyst with more experience compared to most of the green Internet analysts, he should have known better. Apparently not, as is evident in his *BusinessWeek* quote about his overt, subjective cheerleading of the stocks of investment banking clients he dealt with: "What used to be conflict is now a synergy." He shunned his fiduciary duty to be relatively unbiased as an analyst. Grubman's incestuous investment banking behavior destroyed his research credibility. Several of his top recommendations were advocated almost all the way into Chapter 11—Global Crossing, MCI Worldcom, and others. He's now permanently barred from the business.

Analyst compensation, often more than one million dollars annually, is unrelated to the performance of their stock recommendations. A portfolio manager's investment record can be tracked daily in the mutual fund listings. But analysts are not paid for the accuracy of their stock opinions. Their income depends on institutional client polls, overall eminence and influence, institutional sales and trading evaluations, aid in doing investment banking deals (there is still involvement here), and overall subjective judgment by research management.

Opinion Rating Systems Are Misleading

Even if the Street's investment opinions were credible, investors still couldn't determine exactly the meaning of the recommendation. Sometimes Buy means Sell. Brokerage firms have differing stock-rating terminology that can be highly deceptive. Analysts are often forced to hedge, as their investment opinions attempt to straddle dissimilar audiences. Although most firms have contracted their stock opinion format from four or five different gradations to three, there is still excessive wiggle room for hedging. The famous Neutral or Hold monikers are merely a way for analysts to hide and save face, since after the fact they can usually argue that they were accurate, however convoluted the claim. Investors have no clue what to do with such a Hold opinion. Only the highest rating in any firm's nomenclature, usually Buy, Strong Buy, Overweight, and so on, indicates that the analyst has a favorable view on a stock. Or does it?

In the latter part of 2006, according to Barron's, a Morgan Stanley analyst initiated coverage of Toll Brothers with an Overweight rating, the stock trading above $29. Sounds positive, doesn't it? Well, the price target was $23, indicating his expectation of a major drop in price. Apparently, that firm's rating meant only that the stock would do better than its counterparts in the home building industry. This is no help to investors who might have believed the opinion called for a bigger position than the norm, and who could lose that much more money. Confusion reigns.

Analysts use lower-level ratings, such as Accumulate, Above Average, Hold, Neutral, and sometimes even Buy (if the firm has a superior Strong Buy in its system), to convey a negative stance to their key client base, institutional investors. They avoid the more pessimistic classification levels like Below Average, Underweight, Under Perform, or Sell. In order to dodge the flack from corporate executives and those institutional investors who own big positions in the stock. It is also a way to massage investment bankers. Accumulate opinions were once referred to euphemistically as a *Banker's Buy*. Sounds positive, but in reality it's negative. It helps the analyst save face.

When an Opinion Is Lowered from the Peak Rating It Means "Sell"

Any stock rating below the highest level connotes an analyst's pessimism or cautious stance. An analyst opinion change from the top level is tantamount to a literal Sell recommendation. Maintaining the top long-term classification while reducing the near- or medium-term view is another decisive communication of a gloomier opinion. And one should totally disregard all "long-term" ratings. They represent another analyst dodge.

The current almost universal three-level investment rating scheme is fraught with confusion and disparities among different firms. The *Wall Street Journal* asked, in an article discussing a National Association of Securities Dealers (NASD) study, how ratings were applied. "Is an *underperform* stock in an *outperform* industry more attractive than an *outperform* stock in an *underperform* industry?" For sure, the jargon defining investment terms needs to be clearer and more consistent throughout the Street. Does Overweight mean Buy? Recommendations can be absolute or relative. Analysts can cite accuracy with a positive opinion if it outperforms an index or the market, even if the stock declines and investors lose money. An absolute term like Buy might portray an indication the stock may rise anywhere from 10% to 25% in the next 12 months. According to the

Journal article, at Bear Stearns Outperform implies the stock will do better than the analyst's industry coverage. At Smith Barney, a Buy connotes an expected total return of more than 15%. A Buy at UBS Warburg says it's supposed to rise 15% or more over prevailing interest rates. Thankfully, some firms have finally gone to just one investment rating timeframe, eliminating the near-term and long-term tandem that was often a conundrum. But there's a long way to go to get the industry's investment rating systems on a similar page.

It's impossible to determine the level of an analyst's enthusiasm or skepticism from the published rating. Recommendations vary in degree of fervor. Sometimes a Buy is a rather wimpy, weak, low-key endorsement. Other times, a Buy might be a table pounding, jump out of your shoes, immediate action indication. A Hold can be fairly positive, say when the analyst is in the process of gravitating toward a more favorable stance, prior to an upgrade to Buy. Or a Hold could mean the analyst thinks the company's outlook and stock prospects are terrible, but he hesitates to upset vested interests with the dreaded Sell word. The latter is usually the case. The Street normally interprets Hold opinions negatively and so should the individual investor.

Wall Street investment advice is further blemished by being risk adverse. Opinions on stocks are hedged. This obviating is pervasive, stemming from disparate audiences and a mortal fear of being wrong. Sometimes analysts have a Neutral short-term view (this means negative) but a slightly more positive Accumulate or Above Average long-term opinion. That translates into a terrifically negative view, but it's equivocal. If it's a simpler system, the analyst may carry only the Neutral recommendation. That way, he can dodge responsibility no matter how the shares perform. If the stock spirals lower, you'll hear, "I wasn't really recommending it." Conversely, if the shares climb, there'll be nothing but silence. Even Strong Buy ratings carry different degrees of enthusiasm. If the analyst has six or eight companies with the same optimistic opinion, there will be credit taken for those stocks that ascend. A ready excuse is offered, that the name wasn't among the top two or three best picks, for any of those whose prices meander.

The ideal rating system would be a two-pronged scheme to push analysts into one camp or the other. This could be positive/negative, outperform/underperform, or overweight/underweight. Notice my terms for bad stock prospects are less harsh than Sell but indicate essentially the same thing. They aid the analyst and brokerage firm in saving face, and in pacifying relationships with institutional holders and corporate executives. Forget using Buy/Sell—too crass, politically unacceptable. By setting up such a simple system, the analyst view on the stock would be more clearly communicated, and the accuracy more readily tracked. No hedging, no equivocating. But don't expect this to ever happen. Wall Street is not that accountable.

Going a step further, and removing investment ratings altogether, may be advisable for the sophisticated institutional audience. Portfolio managers and buyside (institutional investors) analysts draw their own conclusions and make their own investment decisions. Sellside (brokerage) analyst stock opinions are an annoyance to these investors. Analysts can deliver the same value-added investment research to institutions without this distraction. Research quality and objectivity would improve if analysts no longer felt the pressure of incurring the wrath of big holders and corporate executives when lowering an opinion.

Street investment opinions are also tarnished in other respects. Wall Street loves stocks that are rising now. There is no patience to wait for future upside. It is difficult for an analyst to upgrade a depressed, languishing stock even though it may have a value. It could take too long to move. Once a stock has appreciated and "looks good on the chart," it is much easier for analysts to get all the necessary committee approvals. Such a recommendation is more readily accepted by institutional clients, and there is less risk for the analyst.

As a result, upgrades are usually late, missing much of the rise in the stock. Boosting an opinion requires clear catalysts, evidence, and precise forecasts, all difficult to spell out early. Thus, Buys are rarely value oriented. They are momentum driven. Committees that oversee recommended lists refuse stock suggestions when the price is bumping along the bottom and shows no upside momentum. As a washed-out value, it runs counter to the mentality of the committee. Investors can outwit the Street by seeking stocks that are not in favor or being widely recommended, represent value, and may eventually attract opinion upgrades.

Research Reports Do Not Contain an Analyst's Complete Viewpoint

Because reports are in the public domain and are read by all the disparate audiences that analysts confront, particularly negative or controversial content is watered down, or modulated. The degree of our skepticism, aspects of a company that are unclear but highly suspect, untrustworthy management, lack of confidence in estimates, anything edgy, doubtful, any wariness—none of this gets put into writing. If it did, legal compliance would edit it out anyway. Reports get such scrutiny that analysts are careful; they hold back and reserve the touchier, conjectural content for direct conversations when they can tailor it to a specific institutional client. An analyst's body language or subtle leaning on a stock are never revealed in writing. Although analysts are no longer legally able to hold a radically conflicting stance than the one portrayed in the report, there is much left to be read between the lines.

The Entire Stock Market Is Biased in Favor of Buy Ratings

Think of Wall Street as if it were the auto industry. Automobile companies make cars and trucks. Through their dealers, they sell these products aggressively. Given their vested interest, auto dealers recommend "buy." You've never heard them tell consumers to "sell." An article by Clifford S. Asness in the *Financial Analyst Journal* makes this comparison. He accurately states that, "A large part of Wall Street's business is selling new and used stocks and bonds, which strangely they do make recommendations about." Of course, the Street rarely espouses bearish views on the very products it wants to sell to clients.

Wall Street is totally oriented to a rising market and upward moving stock prices. The common terms used by the Street to describe stock market conditions are heavily slanted toward the positive. When the stock market drops and you lose money in your stock holdings, it's called a "correction." Isn't that absurd? "Volatility" is another term that often surfaces to describe a falling market. Isn't a surging market just as volatile as a declining one? A plummeting market finally bottoms out, and it's seen as "stabilizing," a favorable description. But if stocks are soaring, the market is never portrayed as being unstable. The Street just keeps trying to sugarcoat or neutralize the situation when stocks are not climbing in price.

Institutional investors hold stocks, are long, and rarely sell short or bet on a decline. Most mutual funds and institutions are not allowed to short stocks. Analysts are incentivized to issue Buy opinions by the favorable feedback that flows from major institutional owners of the stocks and from corporate executives. Analysts are discouraged from negative views by the adverse reaction from these constituencies. Sell opinions, especially if in the minority, put us on an unpleasant hot seat.

A *Wall Street Journal* study in early 2004 found the positive bias to be most glaring at smaller brokerage firms that still seem to be in the rut of hyping a lot of Buy recommendations. Even the ten major firms that agreed to several research reforms in a 2003 industry settlement with the New York Attorney General, averaged about twice as many Buy ratings compared to Sells. The ratio was almost seven times more Buys at smaller firms. In a mid-2006 CFA magazine article by Mike Mayo, it was noted that of the recommendations on the ten biggest market cap stocks in the U.S. there were 193 Buys and only six Sells. Systemic bias? I'd say there are vast brokerage investment banking opportunities with these major corporations, subtly swaying analyst opinions. The system is stacked against negative recommendations.

Analysts have an anthropomorphic tendency to fall in love with the companies and stocks that they are advocating. It's like identifying with your captors. Human instinct. The bias is ineffaceable. Some of the insanity has been eliminated and subservience to investment banking is reduced. But don't think for a second that full objectivity has been restored. The percentage of favorable Street recommendations still far outweighs negative opinions, at least if you take published ratings literally. In early 2001, ten months into the precipitous market slide that followed the bubble, Salomon Smith Barney had only one Underperform and no Sells among nearly 1200 stocks it was covering. According to Zacks Investment Research, of the 4,500 stocks it tracked in the fourth quarter of 2005, 42% were rated Buy or Strong Buy. Only 3% carried Sell or Strong Sell recommendations. A research report by a major Street firm in spring 2007 indicated its research department investment rating distribution was 45% Buys, 47% Neutrals, and 8% Sells.

A study by UCLA, UC Davis, and the University of Michigan reveals another form of skewed recommendations. Independent stock research opinions are more accurate than analysts from brokerage firm investment banks. The record was about equal during bull markets when Buy ratings are prevalent. But independents stand out in bad markets when they promulgate more negative views. Brokerage firms are seemingly reticent to downgrade investment banking clients. Gee, why am I not surprised? A brokerage analyst invariably maintains a closer relationship and has more access to executives of an ongoing banking client, creating another positive bias. Studies prove that the analyst at the brokerage that leads an initial public offering of a company, provides noticeably more affirmative coverage than analysts at firms unaffiliated with the deal.

Buy and Sell Opinions Are Usually Overstated

Analysts cheerlead their Buys, and disparage the Sells. The Street tends to overdo its enthusiasm on stocks being strongly recommended, effectively pounding the table to attract investors to amass major positions. The ardor is self-fulfilling. The more proficient analysts are in this endeavor, the higher the stock climbs, and the better our call looks. We promote these favored ideas way out of proportion to the reality, and the stocks can ascend to artificially high, unsustainable levels. The opposite is true for the infrequent Sell opinions. We are overly emphatic on all the negatives, diss the company at every opportunity, and basically pile on an already troubled, depressed stock. This is to help push the shares lower to make our negative view all the more correct. In both situations, analysts overstay their positions. Stocks overreact in both directions far beyond what is warranted by reality, due mainly to analysts going overboard in stressing their stances. Investors should sell when analysts get overly enthusiastic and avoid unloading (maybe even buy) when an analyst has derided a company too long.

Wall Street Has a Big Company Bias

Another bias on Wall Street is an ongoing emphasis on big companies. Analysts have a tendency to focus their coverage on stocks that have the highest market capitalizations. These names are more actively traded and widely held, with the most institutional investor interest. This is where most investment banking business is derived and investment firms generate most of their equity business profits. The bulk of phone calls and press attention pertains to such companies. They are over-covered, over-analyzed, and the price valuations of their stocks tend to be more efficient, fully reflecting all known factors. Technology, telecommunications, and healthcare are the most over-researched, covered by the most analysts. Wall Street tends to add analysts in sectors where it does the most banking and trading business, not necessarily in areas representing the best investments. According to a study by Doukas, Kim and Pantzalis referenced in CFA Digest in mid-2006, there is a clear relationship between excess analyst coverage and stock premiums. The same study showed a direct correlation between low analyst coverage levels and stock price discounts.

Individuals can benefit by making an astute, early investment in smaller companies not already picked over by Wall Street. Mutual funds and other institutions need to take sizeable positions in stocks. Though they may invest in some smaller cap stocks, even a spectacular winner there has minimal influence on a fund's total performance. Therefore, when analysts pound the table on a thinly traded company that proves to be a fine idea, the overall impact is muted. There are meager economics for a brokerage firm in recommending small stocks, whether for trading, banking, or commissions. Brokerage revenues are decidedly boosted by outstanding calls (a rare event) on broadly held stocks, not small caps.

Executives and board members have a similar preference for bigness—they hesitate to do spin-offs, love acquisitions, and are obsessed with company size, enjoying the status of being a part of the S&P 500. But mass usually indicates mediocrity. And mega-mergers never work. Smaller market caps are not emphasized by analysts. Even if a small cap stock is a table pounding Buy recommendation that soars in price, the analyst gets little recognition for being an advocate. Small companies have few shares outstanding and thus only a scant number of investors own the stock and benefit from its appreciation. Most analysts at major firms get attention and make their reputations by emphasizing big cap recommendations. Small stocks present the individual investor with a better prospect of undiscovered value and the potential to achieve greater prominence in the future as their market caps expand.

Brokerage Emphasis Lists Are Frivolous

Most brokerage firms sport their top stock picks in a high-profile emphasis list. These featured rankings are amateur hour. While they often flaunt a statistical case that such Buy collections outperform the market, these "best" recommendations do not perform materially better than all the other favorably rated stocks lacking such exalted status at that firm. Such comparisons are glaringly absent in brokerage research because they are too embarrassing. *Barron's* quantifies the brokers' model portfolio performance every six months using Zacks Investment Research statistics. The record isn't pretty. In 2006, the average brokerage recommended list underperformed the S&P 500. The leader was Matrix USA, not exactly one of the biggest firms on the Street. Over a five-year period, they lagged again, ahead only 44% on average compared to the S&P 500 equal-weighted total return of 69%. The five-year winner was a firm that has no in-house fundamental research analysts—Charles Schwab! What does that tell you?

Like a zephyr, emphasis list ideas blow in and out. Selection committees can be a charade. If they need a new name to add to the exclusive list of best recommendations, the technical chartist might suggest those Buys that have good charts. Analysts in the firm are called and possibilities are trial ballooned. Their decisions are often surprising. The most perplexing aspect is the rather frivolous manner by which these lists are maintained. Assuming a one-year investment time horizon, panic and anxiety can strike these committees when a stock moves a few points. Hip-shooting is common; emotions and stock price charts rule the day. There seems to be no consistent, longer-term, investment-oriented approach. An analyst's best recommendation can be yanked despite protest after falling a few points. Even if it recovers, the name is long gone from the list.

Stock Price Targets Are Specious

Analysts are now required to have price targets on research reports, with attendant justification, which can involve a formal model to calculate fair or intrinsic value. But this also means predicting the future, encompassing influences like overall stock market trends, the economy, war, and interest rates, which are far beyond the analysts' presumably good insight into company and industry prospects. In the bubble years, the Internet analysts pulled absurd, astronomical triple-digit price objectives out of the blue, and naive investors actually gave these goals credence. It still happens, as in the case of the excessive expectations for the Google stock price. In current, more rational times, the guesses may be a bit more tempered but are still unrealistic, or at least unbalanced. Stock price estimates are utilized to emphasize Buy or Sell ratings. Analysts put too high a goal on stocks where they have favorable opinions to help justify their view, and to assist in marketing to hype the story. The price point forecast is artificially low for companies on which analysts are negative. Another issue here is that when such a target is hit, it can trigger a downgrade in analyst opinion. That impacts the stock price and is an adverse short-term influence on long-term investors. Opinion changes based on the stock achieving a published price target should be taken lightly. You can see what I think of price objectives—terrific if you like fiction.

The Street Is Extremely Short-Term in Its Orientation

The modern era of research transformed security analysis and investing, all of Wall Street really, to a shorter, briefer length for everything. Investors can exploit this tendency and enhance portfolio performance by being longer-term oriented, and more patient and value focused. Institutions are entrapped by a quarterly treadmill of performance evaluation. Their investment time horizon has shrunk drastically. If any stock recommendation lacks upside potential in the current quarter, a professional portfolio manager's eyes glaze over. Analysts have succumbed to this same frenzy of near-term expectations and demands. Attention spans are telescoped, so research reports are shriveled in size. Corporations are subsumed by the same trend. Quarterly earnings results are the paramount milestone, a critical influence, the subject of intense analyst emphasis. Annual earnings estimates are dwarfed by expectations for the existing quarter. And it is this short sightedness that gives the individual investor an opening. An individual can really invest and hold stocks for at least two or three years to improve performance results, because they are not being judged on a quarterly basis like the Street.

Wall Street analysts are supposed to be investment analysts doing investment research. That means their conclusions, findings, views, and recommendations are to be investment oriented, having a time horizon of at least a year or two. Yet most institutional clients, particularly the biggest commission producers like hedge funds, are short-term trading oriented. The same for key intermediaries, institutional sales, and the brokerage firms' trading desks that analysts deal with constantly. Mutual fund performance is tracked daily and is measured against the competitors every quarter. Analysts are torn between two conflicting goals. Earnings estimates, price targets, and other prognostications on the companies that analysts cover extend a year or more into the future. But intense pressures mount from clients, traders, and research management for a recommendation to prove out in a period of just days or weeks, months at the longest. This causes Street research to be focused myopically on immediate influences. Analysts are catering to a market of traders rather than a market of investors, and so what they undertake is really trading research. Most Street research is unsuitable for the true, long-term investor.

Research reports and brokerage stock rating systems indicate a one-year investment timeframe. In reality, opinions are based on analyst thinking of how the stock may do over the next one to five months, at the maximum. This stems from the exceedingly short-term trading mentality on Wall Street. If analysts do not believe the stock will take off within the next couple months, there will be no opinion upgrade. The key institutional investor audience seeks instant gratification and is impatient, like the rest of Wall Street. A question I constantly heard was: "What is the catalyst that will move the stock?" When raising an opinion, the Street always stresses the immediate expected development that will drive the price higher. Don't ever think any recommendation is based on how the stock will perform over the next year or two. We get hounded or criticized if our stock recommendation stagnates for even two or three months. Wall Street is not focused on the long-term. Patient investors can outmaneuver Street insiders by a willingness to buy early and hold for a couple years and not be whipsawed by temporary influences.

The short timeframe that defines Wall Street necessitates speed. Analysts are compelled to stress quickness over quality or thoughtfulness. Immediate interpretation of news or events is demanded. Once put forth, the inclination is to stick with that stance, even if later evidence or assessment indicates a different conclusion. Erroneous instant reactions have a way of manifesting over time. Research reports contain mostly reported facts rather than unique, original analysis and inferences. Analysts also love PC-generated earnings models and gravitate toward quantitative aspects. Far more telling is the esoteric, qualitative side to a company's business that is more difficult to evaluate. Such quality security analysis is scant since it takes too long, and analysts are normally in a reactive, hurry up mode.

Analysts Miss Titanic Secular Shifts

This is another consequence of a short-term viewpoint and the herd instinct. Broad industry themes last a while. Major movements like a new technology, a different manufacturing process, or consumer habits that are catalysts for a sweeping industry move are readily identified by the Street once in place and obvious. The trend is underscored as the key underpinning of ongoing recommendations. The problem is that Wall Street always espouses the view that this overwhelming industry effect will endure for the foreseeable future. Inevitably, a critical turning point is eventually reached when the trend begins to subside. But it's subtle. And because analysts are momentum oriented, they rarely see the shift until it's way late. They are too narrowly concentrated on details and do not heed the bigger picture. Analysts are so consumed with marketing, telephone calls, meetings, conference calls, publishing short blurbs, traveling, reacting, and scrambling that there is no time for studied, overall macroassessment. They may be good at evaluating the trees, but they fail to have enough vision to see the forest.

Analysts rarely take seriously the emerging companies that are pioneering a new wave. They are similar to executives who play a defensive game to protect their turf. Established companies rarely create new technologies that make their existing entrenched products obsolete. Analysts also become fixed in their coverage and views, and are predisposed to defend a favorable ongoing opinion of a recognized industry leader. Like the ostrich, they fail to give proper credence to up and coming companies that represent a disruptive market leapfrog. Analysts are uncomfortable with any thinking that might run counter to their long-established point of view. Because the status quo is easier, they often miss the boat when a new force emerges.

The rise of PC software in the late 1980s brought a surge of IPOs, including Microsoft, Lotus Development, and Borland. A friend of mine since elementary school, then an orthopedic surgeon in Ohio, inquired naively whether he should pick up a few Microsoft shares once it started trading. I thought it and a myriad of others—each specializing in spreadsheet, database, operating system, and other PC software—were a speculative flurry and a risky proposition that investors should avoid. Bill Gates' company seemed just like the rest of the bunch, and not that special. And these new companies were challenging the entrenched, established software for larger computers. So I dissuaded my school chum. He could have retired earlier were it not for my foolish advice. I paid only passing attention to this new PC software age. My counterpart at Goldman Sachs, Rick Sherlund, did the Microsoft initial public offering (IPO) and was the early axe in that stock—that is, the most informed analyst covering the name. Within a few years, Microsoft vaulted to the most important and thriving firm of all software and computer services. Sherlund then displaced me as #1 in the vaunted *Institutional Investor* rankings. I paid the price for my oversight.

Street Research Unoriginal, Opinions Similar

Not only is the Street myopic, it is also unoriginal. Everything the Street now publishes or communicates is excruciatingly reviewed for approval. Although research may now be more credible, it is hamstrung, emasculated, and diluted. Pithy, original, or controversial content is difficult to communicate to investors. Analysts run in packs and find standing alone to be uncomfortable. The Street tends to have similar opinions on most stocks. Analysts identify and underscore the macro industry trends in the stock groups covered, which puts them all in the same boat. If the sector is in favor, almost all of us recommend just about every stock. We love a stock when fundamentals are healthy, regardless of excessive valuation. The same is true of the negative side. After major disappointments or shortfalls, we all belatedly change over to negative views. There is little uniqueness or willingness to stand alone from the pack.

Further diminishing the relevance of brokerage investment research and opinion ratings is that research reaches individual investors late. Analyst contact priorities are the sales force and traders, then the press. Stocks react when events occur and news breaks. The analyst first jumps on the squawk box and makes comments to the sales force. Traders get a call about the same time. (They're not supposed to be first, but sometimes they are.) After returning phone calls from institutional sales, the next priority is the press. We love to see our remarks running across the Dow Jones newswire—and Bloomberg, Reuters, and the next day's *New York Times*, too. Then we might start chatting with the key institutional clients like Fidelity. By the time most investors hear of or read our research views, it is way late. Its tardiness renders it worthless for near-term trading. Individual investors are low in the analyst's pecking order and need to treat Street research accordingly.

Analyst Research Is Valuable for Background Understanding

Street security analysts are good for something; they publish expert company and industry research, which is useful for gaining a thorough understanding of the business fundamentals. Research reports detail numerous aspects of a company that provide good background for an investor. Areas such as the earnings outlook, profit forecasts and earning models, business operations, the market, competition, issues and challenges, management, and finances can be readily comprehended by utilizing the reports of research analysts. Such analysts are highly knowledgeable on the industries they cover, and if they have tracked a particular company for a few years, their expertise is deep. Analysts attend briefings for company investors, participate in management conference calls with the Street, and periodically talk with certain executives, such as the chief financial officer (CFO) and director of investor relations (IR). On conference calls, available to all investors to listen in on, analysts ask probing questions, flush out the real story, and are good at exposing critical elements. Because analysts have active contact with executives, they are completely familiar with the company party line, the company's goals and objectives, and its management style. Individual investors are rarely directly privy to this type of information, but this color finds its way into research reports.

Analysts, given their usually steep company and industry expertise, are good at identifying events and influences that could have an impact on a company's outlook. When news breaks or an event occurs, Street analysts can provide detached, cool-headed, informative commentary as to the fundamental effect it might have on a company. This is a common occurrence. A leading competitor in an industry sector has a negative earnings or order rate shortfall. A big acquisition is announced. A blockbuster new product development comes to light. A hurricane or other natural disaster takes place. All these types of news can affect the stock prices of a number of companies. Analysts normally issue reports that shed light and provide an explanation in such circumstances. Often this research is rushed, tends to be a short-term interpretation, and can always be wrong, but it is useful for getting the gist of the situation.

Earnings estimates are another valuable tool contributed by analysts. These are normally accompanied by comprehensive earnings models that indicate forecasts of revenue, operating profit margins, tax rate, cash flow, return on equity ratios, and other such quantitative measures. Earnings projections are both quarterly and annual, and are helpful in assessing the stock price valuation based on the price-to-earnings (PE) ratio. The anticipated rate of growth in profits is an important element in the overall outlook for a company. But the best use of these numbers is in comparing actual results. Stock prices react each quarter to the slightest shortfall or overachievement in results. And they can move precipitously in response to modifications in analysts' earnings forecasts. Sometimes a minor rise indicates materially improving prospects. A trivial reduction can signal notice-ably eroding business conditions. The stock price responds accord-ingly. Single figure estimates tend to cluster together and usually reflect the published management guidance. Still, earnings estimates are a good means for investors to get a handle on Street expectations and the general magnitude of earnings growth.

A Lone Wolf Analyst with a Unique Opinion Is Enlightening

There is serious value added in a unique perspective that is contrary to the crowd. Often there are no hard numbers or evidence to clearly indicate cracks in the surface. A shift to a negative stance that is all alone is a noteworthy signal. Other analysts maintain their favorable views and pooh-pooh the dissenter's conclusion. He is castigated, dissed by executives, attacked by major institutional holders of the stock, and feels like an outcast. These repercussions are anticipated, and that's why a dramatic rating slash is always brutal for the analyst. When an analyst is so courageous and willing to stick his neck out with a minority viewpoint, he is displaying a certain conviction. The view is enlightening, as the justification presents evidence that the preponderance of bullish advocates are wont to admit.

The Best Research Is by Individuals or Small Teams

Individuals and small teams concentrate on a modest range of stocks or a limited segment. Research analyst teams are universal, but the big team approach has been overdone and a shift back toward more individual coverage seems warranted. Teaming enables a far deeper level of detail, earnings models, the nth degree of information, and more immediate response to developments. There are enough bodies to do in-depth reports. The problem is that investors, the sales force, traders, and all the other audiences are unable to absorb this amount of trivia. Analysts get sidetracked, bogged down in all the fine points. It's overkill. Teams are a conundrum for analysts. They both free up senior analyst time from minutiae to ponder bigger picture trends, and also require more attention to details and necessitate oversight, review, coordination, and supervision. The Street is trending toward smaller teams tracking more stocks per person. This is commoditizing research, as analysts are burdened with a greater breadth of coverage. Junior, inexperienced analysts are conducting the research. The heavyweight senior analyst spends most of the time marketing, meeting, and calling on institutions. Analysis is a mile wide and an inch deep. It should be quality, not quantity, that counts.

Analysts may be error prone if they are not concentrating on a narrow industry segment. During my eight-year span at Salomon Brothers in the mid-1980s, I covered the entire computer industry. The mistake was that I, instead of specializing, was attempting too broad a reach. I learned a valuable lesson. I didn't think to specialize in computer services and software until three years after the establishment of a separate category for that sector in the preeminent annual *Institutional Investor* (*I.I.*) analyst poll. Once I made that shift, I immediately vaulted to a #1 ranking and retained *I.I.* All-American team status for 19 straight years.

On the other hand, narrow sector concentration can cause more bias. If analysts cover too few stocks, they have no alternative stocks to recommend when their group sours. While the current Street norm of broader coverage by less-seasoned analysts may leave them open to mistakes, the flaw in the opposite approach is that analysts with a field of coverage that is too limited tend to have a constant positive stance. They can't be left without anything to propose to investors, and institutions do not want to hear negative views on the stock they own.

Overconfident Analysts Who Exhibit too Much Flair Are All Show

Arrogance, showbiz, flair—analysts are noted for these characteristics. They need to demonstrate excessive confidence to the sales force and important institutional clients to display the strength of their convictions. Any hesitation is interpreted as doubt and impacts credibility, just as it affects a politician. We learn quickly to be accomplished

actors, even bluffers. We talk fast, connoting a (false) air of assurance.
The amplitude of our belief in stock recommendations, forecasts, and
assessments varies widely, is sometimes even lacking, but our audience would never know it. And we have such extensive knowledge of
the companies we cover that we are supreme at faking answers to
questions, if necessary, to preserve our omniscient image. This is a
pernicious practice, as investors can be readily swayed, and analysts
might be spectacularly wrong. That was the hallmark of the '90s
Bubble Era.

It should be clear upon realizing Wall Street's well-kept research
secrets that the Street is not a reliable source for objective stock recommendations. That's really not its job. Sure, the Street postures that
it can provide investment advice and financial counsel. But it is structured to trade securities, perform securities transactions, distribute
and sell securities as a dealer, and do corporate finance deals. Wall
Street is not suited to be an investment manager, financial advisor, or
stock selector. In fact, these services that it purports to offer are a
conflict of interest with the bedrock brokerage and banking functions
stated previously. The Street does not intentionally mislead—there is
no deceit—it's just the way the business operates. Therefore, don't
take the Street's directives literally, be aware of its shortfalls, and
invest with the awareness of a Wall Street insider.

2

Understand Wall Street's Misleading Practices

After digesting the ambiguous doubletalk and often deceptive ways of Wall Street discussed in Chapter 1, "Decoding Wall Street's Well-Kept Secrets," investors need to be aware of the more subtle detrimental influences of the Street. Knowing what to discount and putting analysts and their opinions in the proper perspective are key to leveling the playing field. You can outmaneuver even institutional portfolio managers and exploit the Street on a proactive basis by reacting to its propaganda and confusing output the same way as professional insiders.

Wall Street goes on vacation in August (like France), and its the only time there's any possibility to escape with an expectation of minimal business disruption. August has become the norm—things are quiet, the phone doesn't ring, and rarely are there any corporate developments or breaking news. But never think that the Street is dozing. Analysts are always on call. Once I had just arrived on the Amalfi coast at my cliffside hotel in Positano, Italy, early in the afternoon, planning to head for the beach, when the phone rang. My office notified me of a shocking merger of two important companies that I covered, the foremost event in the sector in years. In this situation, an analyst needs to be in the office, with a phone and resources, data, and staff to properly assess the implications. The worst place to wrestle with such a detonation is an isolated beach on the Mediterranean. Analyzing a weighty business matter, like a complex takeover, is brutal when you're in escape mode in paradise. I was consumed all afternoon and evening, sequestered in my hotel room with conference calls, executive discussions, staff deliberations, faxes, dictation, editing...basically a nightmare, a massive disruption to a relaxing holiday.

While I was on a Baltic cruise to St. Petersburg, Russia, a company announced the loss of a massive contract. The shares collapsed, conference calls ensued, and given the time difference, I was up most of the night on the ship's in-room radio telephone. The purser slipped me a phone bill upon debarking at the last port for $5,000. I did a double-take, but my firm was happy to reimburse me that stunning expense, knowing I had worked my ass off during my vacation. It is possible to have some fun on vacations, but the feeling never lasts long. The first day back at the office, my assistant inquired, "Did you have a nice vacation?" She gave me about five minutes to review the trip high-lights before interjecting with, "Well, get over it!" All analysts have such stories. It's the reality.

Street Research Came Full Circle During My Career

The realities of research on Wall Street hit me the first week I arrived at Spencer Trask, a small boutique brokerage firm, in 1971. My shock when discovering the ways of the Street, though, was far transcended by the vast transformation in practices in subsequent decades. I was fortunate to evolve as a securities analyst during the 1970s, an era when Street research was just beginning to emerge. At that time, it took years for an analyst to establish credibility and make an impact on institutional investors. I trudged along. My firm sent me to public speaking training sessions. Over a three-year span, requiring intensive reading, studying, and an annual all-day exam, I obtained a Chartered Financial Analyst (CFA) designation. That seemed to be *de rigueur* for a career analyst at the time. My director of research was a Yale English major, so my reports at first were heavily edited. They finally became readable, intelligible. My nickname was "Hound of the Baskervilles." I'm not sure why, maybe imputing tenacity and assiduity. We analysts did everything ourselves: meetings, reports, executive interaction, analysis, client contact, and sales force dialogue. I was a one-man band. There were no teams. It made for a complete analyst.

The brokerage firm that I joined was typical of the dozens of flourishing, stock-focused, research-based partnerships then so prevalent in the business. Our office was located a few doors down from the New York Stock Exchange, like all other brokerage headquarters, in the heart of Wall Street. Since then, most of the firms have moved uptown. Spencer Trask was classy, genteel, professional, and quiet, having been in business since 1853. I found the cadre of research analysts there to be intelligent, probing, thoughtful, and proficient writers. They spent most of their time conducting research, talking to executives, visiting the companies they covered, and composing in-depth reports. There was little financial or mathematical analysis, only modest attention paid to detailed modeling in that pre-PC period. Most firms like mine did no investment banking and no trading. Research generated the revenue and was not beholden to multiple, conflicting constituencies. Analysts were objective and the research was credible. Securities analysts were not prominent figures in the media, but rather more akin to surgeons or Ph.D professors. Individual retail clients were fairly important, and paid fat commission fees for their stock transactions, so at weekly research meetings some of the commentary encompassed individual investment considerations. Another startling observation, certainly by today's standards, was the leisurely pace of activity—arriving for work at 9 AM and departing at 5:15 PM, with long client lunches and sometimes dinners.

Individual clients were taken seriously by the firm, but I quickly found that institutional clients received most of the analysts' attention. Another revelation, something I hadn't realized before reaching the Street, was that stocks were assessed based primarily on the future earnings prospects, a given to insiders, but something I did not realize before reaching the Street. And corporate executives were inclined toward wooing analysts for favorable opinions. This was often done by extending perks such as IT&T's annual all-expense paid analyst trip to Paris with spouses to hear management briefings.

(Largess like this is no longer allowed due to changes in securities regulations.) Compensation was modest by later standards. Established senior analysts averaged $50,000-$100,000.

The stock market was in the doldrums during much of the 1970s, tanking for almost three straight years during 1972–1974 and remaining dull for most of the rest of the decade. Until 1975, there were excessive, fixed commissions that paid for research without the help of other brokerage income sources like trading or investment banking. And research wasn't that costly; I started out in 1971 with an MBA and didn't achieve the $100,000 income level until 1980. My daughter Laurel was born during my first few years on the Street, I had a mortgage, and my son Justin showed up six years later. Finances were tight. Those were lean times for a junior analyst.

The research process encompassed spending chunks of time questioning and having discussions with company executives. Certain executives were just unavailable to analysts. H. Ross Perot, the founder of EDS, was one such figure. I was the only Wall Street representative at EDS's October Monday night annual meeting in Dallas. It was a friendly audience of employees and spouses. Information flowed. But the climax was dinner later at Perot's house for the management team. I was invited along and got to know his children, ogle his Monets, and schmooze with all the other executives and their wives. One year, the NFL Monday Night Football game featured the Cowboys at home at the same time as the annual meeting, a scheduling crisis for most of the EDS executives that were season ticket holders. That pushed the gathering to a Thursday night slot the next year.

My firm merged with a mid-sized wire house, Hornblower & Weeks, a brokerage that catered mainly to retail individuals with essentially no interest in research. The good analysts fled to other firms. Salomon Brothers, a prestigious, high-profile, aggressive, institutional firm on Wall Street at that time, hired me as the computer industry analyst in 1977. My honeymoon as an emerging analyst was over. The protected, cozy camaraderie I had been used to was now a quaint memory. The floor traders in "the room" (the biggest brokerage trading floor on Wall Street) ran Salomon Brothers, and I immediately learned to tether myself to the head equity trader, feeding him trading angles on the computer stocks a couple times a day. This aspect was colorfully portrayed in Michael Lewis's book *Liar's Poker*.

I soon began to bolt out of analyst meetings in mid-session and run to the payphones to reach our traders if I sensed news aspects that might impact a stock. That was before cell phones. At Salomon Brothers I became attuned to working closely with the trading desk. Most firms hadn't yet thought of having their analysts aid traders. I was early in this now commonplace practice.

The research department at Salomon started to gravitate to conventional stock coverage. I was the first there to publish a company report, as opposed to industry analysis, a breakthrough at the firm. Henry Kaufman was Salomon's noted economist in the early 1980s. He had a worldwide following and the clout to move markets with his interest rate forecasts. Kaufman led the entire stock market out of the 1970s doldrums with his dramatic prediction of an interest rate shift in 1982. He was a senior player at Salomon, but took the time to tediously monitor my ground breaking initial report, a scary tactic for that trading firm.

When I arrived, Mike Bloomberg, the head equity trader, had just moved off the desk to a position of back office tech support. He soon developed sophisticated bond data tracking terminals and software. When Salomon merged into another trading firm, Phibro, Bloomberg was outta there. Within a few years, his new company, Bloomberg L.P., became a household name on the Street and his financial data service was ubiquitous. He chuckled all the way to the bank. I ran into him on the beach in the Hamptons once and his first question was, "McClellan, are you still writing all that bullshit?" He was forthright and facetious. He got some comeuppance years later when we both flew in F-16s with the Air Force, both of our stomachs going through convulsions. Afterwards, he, like me, was green and staggering. He's now the mayor of New York City.

The early 1980s was about the time that all Street analysts started to become more involved with the investment banking function, eventually leading to the downfall of objective research in the 1990s. A sweeping management shift occurred at Electronic Data Systems (EDS), a stock I covered closely, launching Mort Meyerson as its driving force under H. Ross Perot. Over the next few years, I made several trips with the EDS management team to meet with institutional investors. My association with EDS was mainly research related, and not the blindly biased cheerleader role that became prevalent in the '90s Bubble Era. But Salomon was instrumental in

EDS's acquisition by General Motors, and I was engaged in numerous investment banking deals with EDS over the years. This was the dawn of the analyst role in banking.

While at Salomon I got the bug to write a book about the computer industry, its future prospects, the companies, the managements, and my views. This was a crazy concept because if I was forthright a tumult of controversy would follow, dwarfing the consequences of a negative research report. A book carries greater validity than reports and its impact is more powerful. And so it was with *The Coming Computer Industry Shakeout*, which hit the bookstores in June 1984.

I went about interviewing the CEOs of the 50 leading computer industry companies, starting with John Opel, Chairman of IBM. Doors swung wide open when CEOs were informed I was undertaking this book project, which was a side benefit to an analyst covering the industry. I labored in my basement starting at 4 AM each workday, scribbling in longhand on yellow pads, before heading to the office at 6:30 AM. On the weekends, I started at 6 AM. I started drinking coffee for the first time in my life. The heat was on to publish before my material became obsolete. Upon getting my hands on the first printed copy of the book, I had an emotional reaction, an unusual experience for me, because I'm a guy, and we rarely incur any real feelings. I took it to bed with me and cuddled it all night. The book was part of me. I had just given birth.

The book was conceived in the library of the QE2 on a Caribbean cruise. I presented the finished product to the captain in a reception line a year later on another QE2 voyage. Our dining room waiter handed me a note the next morning, inquiring if we'd like to switch to the Captain's table for the duration. Wondering who might also be sitting there, another scribble arrived at the next meal from the British server indicating Stan Musial, Brooks Robinson, and a couple other baseball Hall of Famers. The English waiter asked, "Who are those people?" As a lifelong baseball fan, I almost passed out in delirium, incredulous at the opportunity to schmooze with these heroes for the next eight days. I gasped and stuttered an affirmative reply.

Shakeout made more waves than I expected. It hit some bestseller lists and was favorably reviewed and advertised in the *Wall Street Journal*, *New York Times*, and other papers. TV interviews ensued, and I was a guest on Lou Rukeyser's *Wall Street Week*. One marketing-oriented CEO purchased three dozen books, had me sign notes to him in each, and bestowed them on his best customers, claiming that each was his own single personal copy. A storm of contention arose from the companies in the book on which I made negative or critical comments. Two or three even threatened legal suits.

Security analysis progressed in the 1980s to what is recognized today as institutional research. The research became more sophisticated, detailed, specialized, focused, prolific, and timely, and began to emanate from teams of analysts rather than stand-alones. Analyst coverage narrowed in order to be more thorough. This evolution coincided with the trend toward dominance of institutions and their insider advantage. It was the end of any pretense of a level playing field for the individual investor. The game became complex. Analysts were consumed by institutional investors, research became convoluted, and individual investors were abandoned.

My arrival at Merrill Lynch in the mid-1980s coincided with a research buildup by major brokerage firms all over Wall Street. The leading firms started hiring analyst all-stars. The influence of the *Institutional Investor* poll rankings skyrocketed. I reached the #1 slot amongst my competitors in my sector of coverage and was involved in taking Oracle, Fiserv, First Data, Accenture, and other such companies public. Analysts started having more widespread impact on stocks as well as contributing more heavily to brokerage profits. But security analysts were not yet media darlings, not recognized household names.

In the early 1990s I shifted my location to San Francisco. That period was the start of the Street's push to build technology analyst teams in the Silicon Valley region. Analyst power and status surged. Their compensation soared as the decade progressed. Technology analysts reigned supreme, especially once the Internet bubble began to inflate. I built a team, held bustling conferences in Miami Beach, published volumes, made my share of TV appearances, and traveled from the Pacific Rim to Italy, Scotland to Australia to meet with institutional clients. However, as the Internet exhilaration blossomed, my coverage of mundane, profitable, solid computer services stocks was viewed as having missed the boat, not part of the Internet action. Later, after the bubble had burst, institutions flooded back to the safe, low-key, reliable computer services stocks and I was back in favor.

Research was respected at the beginning of the decade but discredited by the end. During the '90s Bubble Era analysts were worshipped like rock stars. Amateur investors, startup company CEOs, even institutional investors and the press exalted analysts as the new alchemists. But quality, impartial, thoughtful research was degraded by a thousand cuts. After widespread corporate earnings shortfalls, steep stock price declines, and pervasive wrong investment opinions, the damage was done. As the bear market accusations and scandals ensued, analysts were cast as villains. Following the 2000 stock market crunch, people were often aghast when I told them I was a Wall Street analyst. It was as if I were a scoundrel, similar to offenders like Henry Blodget in the dot-com era and rogues like Jack Grubman in the telecom bonanza. Street research began its descent as the new millennium emerged and has continued in a downward spiral ever since.

Now that you have been introduced to some of Wall Street's secrets and have a grasp on the evolution of research over the decades as reflected by my career, you need the graduate course in comprehending Wall Street's misleading practices. Individual investors cannot invest properly until they discount the research directives from the Street. Beyond filtering out incessant Street noise, you must put Street research in the proper perspective.

Research Is Centered on Institutional Clients, Not Individual Investors

For almost two decades now, analyst attention has been directed to institutions, not individual investors. Retail clients are a low priority on Wall Street. The individual investor is an afterthought, mostly neglected by analysts and research departments. Research for individual investors is tepid. In many instances, research is simply repackaged, abbreviated, and watered down—you might say dumbed down—for retail clients. That makes it even more difficult to glean the nuances of an analyst's thinking by reading research reports. An analyst's ultimate judgment on stocks is communicated verbally in a tailored manner to portfolio managers, but seldom, if ever, directly to individual investors. Analysts rarely talk to the office managers or the biggest retail brokers at their firm, and almost never do they have contact with registered reps in branch offices. Most analysts totally avoid these financial consultants' calls. Given the low position retail has in the long chain (traders, institutional sales, press, institutional investors, corporate contacts—all precede individual clients in analyst priority), most investment ideas are shopworn by the time a report is read by an individual investor.

Private individual investors, served by the financial consultant sales force or brokers, need unbiased, black and white, definitive, opportune Buy and Sell opinions. They want the analyst to be a stock picker or a portfolio manager. They expect to be able to follow analyst investment ratings literally, have the stock price targets be credible, and trust that the analyst's research is oriented to their objectives. The wish list is nice, but one that is only a pipe dream. Most of an analyst's time is spent marketing, not doing research. That means communicating investment views and information in direct conversations with institutional type investors, such as mutual fund portfolio managers. The consuming orientation is with portfolio managers and analysts at the mutual funds, banks, insurance companies, hedge funds, pension funds, and other institutions. The practice got the Street into trouble after the 1990s bubble finally burst. Private retail clients had been misled by taking analysts' stock opinion ratings too literally. They really thought a Buy rating meant the analyst viewed the shares as attractive. Wrong.

You need to know that your place as an individual investor in the Wall Street pecking order is the bottom of the totem pole. Outside of the brokerage firm, institutional clients hold sway. Analysts are beholden to these giant investment pools, and can be manipulated by them. Because the biggest institutional investors are the brokerage firms' prime clients, they have titanic leverage over the Street. These organizations have portfolio managers making stock selections and don't need Wall Street analysts for that purpose. In fact, when holding several million shares of a stock, you can visualize their reaction to a Street downgrade that drives the price several points lower. Even the classiest institutional clients vilify us for damaging their performance. That reaction is a key influence inhibiting analysts from reducing opinions or having negative ratings.

Analysts spend double or triple the time on institutional client contact compared to research analysis. And the institutional audience gets essentially 100% of an analyst's marketing attention compared to individual investors. They play almost exclusively to institutions like Fidelity, Putnam, Wellington, Citigroup, T. Rowe Price, Alliance, American Express, Capital Research, and to the hedge funds that trade so actively. The time devoted to institutional marketing detracts enormously from doing research. Travelling to curry their favor takes analysts not only to major cities around the globe, but also to Des Moines, Topeka, Salt Lake City, Vancouver, Portland, Madison, Lansing, Raleigh, Tallahassee, Montgomery, Indianapolis, Chattanooga, Nashville, and Memphis—not your usual everyday haunts. We go the extra mile, and expend enormous energy, not for individual investors, but for that all-important commission allocation vote from the institutions. These organizations allocate vast commission dollars to the brokerage firms for analyst research support to their portfolio managers and own in-house research.

Institutions make constant demands on analysts, insisting we bring managements of the companies we cover to their cities for meetings, requiring exclusive one-on-one executive meetings at our conferences, and pressing us to call them first with insightful tidbits and subtle opinion shadings. Their every whim is made a priority. Fidelity or a huge hedge fund gets one of the earliest calls from the analyst after he hangs up with his trader and a couple of institutional salespeople. Analysts are sucked into a vortex. Institutional power far transcends mere analysts. Commission revenue and transaction flow influences the brokerage firms' profits, the trading room floor activity, and investment banking IPO and other financing deals. Teutonic plates have shifted, and Wall Street is now consumed by these institutional clients, leaving the individual investor far behind.

Despite the general neglect of individual investors by most of the Street, the main research offered to them is commentary on strategic market direction and the economic outlook. Analysts are commonly coerced to align their industry and company outlook with the firm's economic scenario. The only problem is that economists are useless. I cannot tell you how many times the economists at brokerage firms flip-flop their forecasts, following and reacting to events. We cannot blame our bad stock calls on a faulty forecast by the in-house economist. Smart analysts totally disregard such predictions lest they be whipsawed in different directions and made to look silly. In early

2004, for example, Street economists virtually all anticipated a monthly gain of 150,000 in employment. The number came out at 1,000, and the stock market nose dived. A *Wall Street Journal* article said it all, alluding to their "big staffs, sophisticated models, reams of historical data, and degrees from known schools...and still they forecast about as well as groundhogs."

Wall Street Largely Disregards Market Strategists and Technical Analysis

Market strategists are not helpful in making money in the market. Their track record is mixed. Strategists are always fascinating and entertaining, and they convey insightful investing observations and chatter on market direction. But they tend to be big picture and are as biased as security analysts. Even more so than analysts, most of these experts run in packs. If they are bearish for too long, their brokerage firms get antsy and push them out the door. This has happened several times. So if their job security is important to them, strategists will not maintain a negative overall market posture for long. Research strategists rarely tell the analyst when they decide to label any of his stocks attractive or gloomy—and if we wait a month, their view changes. Good analysts can never hide behind the strategists' forecasts. Since strategists are superfluous in attracting investment banking clients, they have now been relegated to a lower status on Wall Street.

Technical analysis is only correct about half the time. Such commentary on historic patterns and market relationships is interesting but is always hedged and of no help in making astute investment decisions. Past stock price patterns are of little aid in forecasting the future. Technical analysts are Delphic, often creating more confusion than clarity. Analysts and most insiders pay no attention to conjectures by these prognosticators.

Insiders Give Little Credence to Favorable Stock Opinions

If big picture forecastive research is of little consequence, so are most Buy recommendations. Ongoing Buy ratings are often stale. There is reticence to downgrade. Analysts keep their Buy recommendations too long, enamored with momentum winners. It is tough for us to downgrade an opinion based on excessive valuation alone, even if the stock is grossly overpriced, as was glaringly evident in the 1990s bubble. Analysts need hard facts and events to justify a downgrade. As a result, by the time there is enough evidence like earnings shortfalls or a drop off in orders to make an obvious, visible case for a downgrade, it is too late and the share price has already fallen. A metals analyst I knew in the 1980s had a Strong Buy on LTV, a steel producer, the day it filed Chapter 11—a notable embarrassment. Analysts are carried along by market and industry trends, yet are so myopically focused on specific companies that they miss the inflection point when the industry sector business fundamentals start to moderate. Our momentum nature constrains us from shifting an opinion when we first begin to sense some issues emerging that give us pause.

Analysts are reticent to downgrade opinions, fearing institutional holder retaliation. Buyside analysts and portfolio managers are most generous in voting commission allocations to the firms of the sellside analysts that help tout their stocks. These institutions vent their fury and banish brokerage analysts who downgrade ratings on the stocks they hold. This anticipated punishment is a critical constraint when pondering an opinion reduction.

We come under so much criticism for reducing ratings that our argument must be airtight. Yet it is discomforting to reduce an opinion after the stock has already started to fade. This creates hesitation. Like the monkey that sees no evil, we close our eyes to initial negative developments. By the time the weight of negative evidence is exceedingly compelling, most of the damage to the stock has already been done. When analysts finally capitulate and go to a full-blown Sell opinion, the stock has likely already hit rock bottom. Although patience may be required, there is usually more upside potential in the shares at that juncture than further downside vulnerability.

Brokerage firms have made the procedure of altering an investment rating hugely more complex for the analyst because of regulatory and legal issues, and the consequence of the pathetic stock recommendation record once the 1990s bubble had burst. Investment research committees meet at certain intervals, require burdensome reports and documentation, grill the analyst, and then legal/compliance gets involved. There is a lot of second guessing and attention paid to current stock price trends, rather than a longer-term investment time horizon. Changing an investment opinion is a frustrating exercise. And the analyst needs to be ensconced in the office to jump through all these hoops—forget being on the road somewhere. It's just easier to do nothing. Opinion changes are hardly worth all the effort. Analysts thus resist upgrades and downgrades. Ratings thay may be inappropriate are left there out of inertia.

Early stock opinion downgrades are both infrequent and anguishing. Taking a negative stance and lowering an opinion is like a divorce—it may be necessary, but it certainly is unpleasant. Because it is so challenging to be the first analyst on the Street to undertake an opinion reduction, investors may find these dramatic calls effective, if coming from a veteran analyst highly credible in covering the stock. After more than 16 years of superb execution and fabulous stock performance, EDS laid an egg in 1996, almost immediately after regaining its independence in a spin-out from General Motors. The company's quarterly earnings results ran across the newswire, vastly below Street expectations. My instinct told me something was terribly amiss, and my reaction was immediate. In this case, there was no prolonged torment, no deliberations, or committee meetings, or searching. I summarily downgraded it with no time to ponder the consequences. It was an emotional, traumatic situation and, given my reputation and prolonged bullish view on the stock, it had a primordial impact. The company and its shares performed pathetically over the ensuing three years. This rating drop happened so abruptly that it was actually easier to effect than most reductions. But even this good call was after the fact; the bad news had already hit. That was more than ten years ago. In this new era of heavy compliance oversight, such a quick reaction and opinion change is rare or impossible.

Smaller Capitalization Companies Suffer Benign Neglect

Analysts and institutional investors' focus their attention on large companies and big cap stocks. They also heavily favor growth stocks that usually carry high PE multiple valuations. That's what makes them big cap stocks. Not only Street analysts, but also Goliath mutual funds, concentrate heavily on the big names. They tend to ignore the massive array of smaller companies that can achieve good growth for decades before maturing or maxing out their market. Countless studies reveal the stunning outperformance of small cap value stocks compared to large cap growth stocks since the 1920s. The difference is off the charts. A *New York Times* article reported a *Financial Analysts Journal* study showing such small caps outdistancing the big caps by a factor of 100 times from 1926 to the present. Yet Street research analysts and most institutions are unable to emphasize this attractive segment.

Under-followed stocks on Wall Street generally outperform those that get heavy attention and a multitude of research coverage. The Street tracks big cap stocks to generate more trades. Big caps are where institutional clients are concentrated and investment banking does business with those firms. So, these highly trafficked names are overexploited and well-discovered. A major Street firm assessed some 40 investment strategies it had put forth in 2006. The best one was investing in the stocks that had the least analyst coverage. According to Barron's, the 50 stocks in the S&P 500 followed by the fewest analysts in 2006 had a 24.6% gain vs. a 13.6% advance in the entire S&P 500 index.

The best recommendation of my entire career was a small cap stock. I was instrumental in the initial public offering of Fiserv in 1986, and it was a Buy recommendation almost constantly until I retired. It provided financial market computer services and compiled an incredibly consistent growth record. The executives were solid and trustworthy Midwesterners. Fiserv was a stellar stock for more than 15 years. Paychex was another small cap name that I identified early. As the biggest player specializing at the low end of the payroll processing market (its average client had 11 employees) it had established a dynamic growth record, impressive profit margins, and a stalwart balance sheet. Competitors could not touch it. The company was able to generate a profit from a one-person payroll client. The chairman and founder was a playful bachelor at the time who, on occasion took Las Vegas by storm and ran for governor of New York. But he managed the company the old-fashioned way: quantitative targets, a narrow specialization, cash generation, and organic growth. I staked my reputation on the stock with a Strong Buy. It performed fantastically. I rode this horse for years, and it's now a big cap. These are examples of how good small cap stocks can perform for decades.

Analysts Are Young, Unseasoned, and Lack Historical Judgment

The length of time an analyst has covered a stock is key. It takes a seasoned perspective, gained over a long period of time, for an analyst to accurately judge a company's prospects. Street insiders only respect veteran analysts covering a sector over an extended period. The analyst needs to see how a firm reacts in bad times, observe its practices in boom times, view management in different situations, and live through industry cycles. Company executives can be caught up with current events and have minimal long-term perception. Analysts, like consultants, must bring experienced time-tested historical knowledge to bear on any company evaluation. If an analyst has only been covering a stock for two or three years, it is insufficient; 10 years is more appropriate. I covered some stocks like Automatic Data and EDS for more than 30 years. My insight was frequently superior to executives who had not participated over the decades in the company's varying conditions.

It's stunning to me how many leading Wall Street analysts have had less than 10 years experience on the Street. The three-year bear market from 2000–2002 and plummeting compensation pushed veterans into retirement, management, or over to the buyside. Senior analysts have moved on. The average analyst age has tumbled. Without historical perspective, Street analysts are subject to falling into the same trap that occurred with the absurd extremes and bad judgment of the 1990s. Firms painted with red ink were going public. Stock prices relative to earnings were infinite. Self-serving commendatory bias was rampant. But two and a half years after March 2000, the NASDAQ had nose-dived 78%. Analyst recollection of the '90s Bubble Era excesses was already dim. Forget about any tempering influence from distant occurrences like the 18 consecutive years from 1966–1982 when the Dow Jones Average stagnated in a narrow range, a depressing state of no progress. Street research analysts today have little institutional memory of these types of conditions.

Since 2000, the number of Wall Street analysts has diminished by 40%, and the total is expected to fall by another 30% or more by 2008, according to the Tabb Group research firm, as pointed out in *Barron's*. Research budgets have been slashed by more than 40% as the main source of funding, commissions, have been cut in half since 2000. Brokerage research is being impacted by a deteriorating business model. Conversely, in-house institutional investor buyside research spending is climbing. Brokerage firms are managing stock coverage by assigning more companies to fewer analysts, or at least cheaper, less-experienced analysts. Compensation has diminished and so has expertise.

My retirement at age 60, after 32 years as an analyst, was a seminal event because it is extremely rare for an analyst to last more than a decade or two. Many high-profile analysts do not have MBA degrees or Chartered Financial Analyst (CFA) designations. The brain drain started in 2000 as analysts fled to hedge funds. In the 1980s and 1990s, smart, ambitious graduate students pursued MBAs and headed to Wall Street. Now most of these great minds have gone off to the institutions that perform investing functions like private equity firms, hedge funds, or venture capital. Intelligent, creative, insightful analysts are scarce. The brilliant graduates are branching into more promising fields. Analysts now have little sense of history. Judging corporate executives is a key ingredient in evaluating stocks, and to develop this skill takes 10 or 20 years of observation. Youthful analysts can be misled by rarified access to top executives. They can be hard-working, intelligent, knowledgeable, and good communicators, but there is no substitute for years of seasoning.

Deletion of Stock Coverage Is a Red Flag of Caution

Dropping stock coverage is often subtle—the Street downplays the move—but it is telling. Analysts rarely walk away from following a winning company that has a promising outlook. Dropping coverage is a graceful method of avoiding an unpleasant downgrade. I remember an experience I had with HBO & Co., a languishing, troubled company in healthcare computer services, when it hired an impressive, smooth, hotshot new CEO to commence a turnaround. After monitoring the progress for a couple years, I finally added it to coverage with a Buy rating. The business was heavily software based, and quarterly bookings drove the numbers. There was only modest visibility but terrific momentum as the company expanded its sales force, moved into adjunct markets, and made acquisitions. Quarterly earnings were sparkling.

Then I began to develop a sense of uneasiness. Acquisitions blurred the operating results. The company's size made it a challenge to sustain the high growth that executives were forecasting and investors anticipated. Competitors' results were lackluster. Its earnings growth and profit margins were vastly superior to its counterparts in the business. Like WorldCom demonstrated a few years later, this contrast can be a telltale sign. Software orders and related revenue can be variable on a quarterly basis, but HBO's results were smooth as silk, despite minimal recurring revenue to aid stability. It made me suspicious and uncomfortable. I decided to stop following it in the process of reorienting my coverage emphasis. It was a graceful way to avoid the agony of either lowering an opinion or continuing coverage and risk the company hitting the wall. Sure enough, later on, after being acquired for a huge price of $14 billion, it was discovered that numerous sales were fictitious and fraudulent. Four members of top management have pleaded guilty so far in criminal cases, and the chairman has been indicted. This was the best negative call I never had to make.

A Glaring Lack of Coverage May Indicate Skepticism

When all the analysts tracking a certain sector follow a stock or a sub-grouping and one analyst avoids that coverage, it probably connotes his doubts. This situation is another version of a dissenting negative opinion. Take note. Analysts take some heat when the shares of a stock that all the others cover are soaring and it appears he has missed the boat by not following or advocating it.

It's nerve-wracking to appear to be an ostrich. Investors thought I had finally lost it by not staying on the leading edge as markets shifted and a new era emerged in the 1990s: Internet eBusiness consulting

firms. The Street viewed it as a crossroads that I had not properly recognized. The sentiment emerged that I was a dinosaur. Other analysts
recommending these names focused on revenue growth, new client
additions, and futuristic trends since the companies bled red ink and
had essentially no profit potential for the foreseeable future. Analysts
had little historic perspective on prior bull market excesses, technology
boom-busts, or obscenely overvalued investments.

The sector was Internet-based, demand was off the charts, and the
expansion was meteoric. It was "the new thing." Investors viewed the
firms in the sector as the new alchemists. Some of the stocks hit triple
figures before their oblivion. I was on Wall Street during a euphoric
period in the 1970s and, as a history follower, had read books like
Extraordinary Popular Delusions and the Madness of Crowds and
Kindleberger's *Manias, Panics, and Crashes*. I had a seasoned perspective. These Internet-based companies were dazzling, curious, and
exciting, but as investments they were incredulously speculative, with
nothing but red ink. All the eBusiness consulting stocks subsequently
disappeared into a massive abyss. Most of the analysts promoting the
eBusiness stocks were fairly junior, and almost all have now disappeared from the business. I rode out the debacle unscathed—and
later pundits quipped that I had come back into fashion.

Insiders Attempt to Leap Ahead of Upgrades

An analyst may be leaning more positively toward a particular stock
but not yet upgraded it to a Buy. The first indication is a change in the
rating from Underperform or Sell, up to a Neutral or Hold. Sometimes the less-negative leaning may be detected in the research commentary on a Hold rated stock. The best investment opportunity is
not what an analyst is currently recommending. That's yesterday's
news and is already fully reflected in the stock price. The stock has
probably been a Buy for a while, and other analysts are likely pushing
it too. Insiders seek the stock that carries a Neutral or Hold opinion
but seems imminent to be upgraded to Buy.

Analysts are looking for indications of light at the end of the tun-
nel or some early signs of recovery. Any such positive signals, and the

evolution will begin toward a more favorable view. At an early stage with scant evidence, it's premature for an analyst to shift the formal rating. But we always have inclinations, feelings that there is potential, so we monitor developments. There is little downside in maintaining a Hold opinion if steady improvement does not unfold. If there is headway for a few months, the seeds are sown for an upgrade to Buy. When a Street recommendation shifts from Sell to Neutral or Hold, it's a good buying opportunity, before the opinion moves up to Buy. You might say in that case, "Hold means Buy."

Institutional Investor Poll Rankings Warp Research

The stature, influence, impact, reputation, and compensation of Wall Street analysts are heavily determined by their annual ranking on the *Institutional Investor* magazine All-Star Team poll results each October. Analysts are compelled to amass *I.I.* votes during the spring each year when the poll is being conducted among the client base of institutional investors. *Institutional Investor* votes and annual poll position are a primary analyst aim, supplanting objective, quality research, investor service, stock picking, and most other research goals. The power and influence of *Institutional Investor* rankings transcends virtually all other research objectives. The compensation for analysts landing in the top three positions in their category is essentially akin to professional sports all-stars. Year-end evaluation is skewed to this measure. Gaining a high *Institutional Investor* standing is a primary goal for analysts, as opposed to it being a byproduct indicator. It corrupts research, taints the process, and skews analyst efforts, as evidenced by the superstar analysts and egomaniac attitudes which manifest in the sorry '90s Bubble Era.

Analysts often embark on unusual, high-profile endeavors to attract the attention of mutual funds, banks, and other such institutional voters. A dramatic opinion upgrade is used as an artifice to curry favor with major holders or attract notice from potentially interested investors. But don't be drawn in. Street insiders discount any flamboyant opinion upgrades during April–June. It's just electioneering. Such recommendation changes need to be put in perspective. They are not necessarily erroneous, but the catalyst behind the action is questionable and timing is suspicious.

In contrast, rating downgrades are avoided like the plague during this period. Analysts do not want to raise the ire of institutional holders by attacking a stock during this critical voting stretch. They postpone such unpleasant actions until the polls are closed. Be prepared for a mini-flurry of catch-up downgrades during late June or in August. July is earnings reporting time, and it may be awkward and risky to lower an opinion just ahead of results. An analyst might appear to have inside information or may be immediately proved off beam, which is a consummate embarrassment. To avoid this peril, analysts ease rating reductions in under the rug, during the August vacation month, hoping to go unnoticed.

It's insane to think that a professional industry trade magazine's annual research rankings are a central driving factor for almost all analysts, but career achievement and year-end bonuses are critically weighted by placement in this poll. These standings generate widespread publicity and are noticed by the chairman and all other management in the firm. The entire investment industry, the press, and even the public exalt "All-Star" team members. High-profile All-Star team status is swayed heavily by analyst marketing and communications as opposed to the quality and accuracy of the research. It's like the movie studios' over-the-top advertising and lobbying for their best films early each year in order to obtain Academy Award nominations. Analysts do the same thing to enhance their *Institutional Investor* standings. It's all about marketing and is counterproductive to research.

Owing to this *I.I.* voting in late spring, January to May is a period of research frenzy. Brokerage investor conferences are almost all conducted during this span. Most analysts jam in several executive road shows to meet with institutional clients during these months. Analyst marketing trips around the country are double or even triple the amount done in the fall. In addition, industry studies, dramatic opinion changes (usually favorable), and other such special research endeavors are cranked up during this timeframe. Phone calls to heavyweight, influential institutional clients skyrocket. All of this is legitimate, value-added information, but it is trumped up and delivered in abnormally high volume in an artificially concentrated period.

Institutional Investors Get Preferred Treatment

Mammoth institutions demand preferential Street treatment. The big enchiladas on the buyside often demand one of the earliest if not the first telephone call in order to glean the nuances from an analyst who puts out a new pronouncement or observation on the morning sales force conference call. The institutional sales desk usually hits the analyst with key priority call assignments to discuss such research assertions. These gorilla clients have power to demand the best executive one-on-one timeslots at brokerage conferences, special conference call briefings to their portfolio manager teams, preferred meetings with analysts during a day of marketing in their city, and the analyst's aid in scheduling calls and meetings with top corporate executives. They commonly ask analysts about which stocks they are "becoming more excited about" or "starting to get more concerned about." This can be in the company of a brokerage firm's heavyweight salespersons who can influence analyst compensation with their year-end evaluations. The pressure is extreme to give privileged insight and treatment to these institutions while the small individual investor is getting screwed.

Major Buyside Institutions Have Access to Selective Information

Big institutions have closed-door, exclusive access to executives. Demand by major institutional stockholders for cozy one-on-one meetings with corporate executives is rampant and an entrenched routine. Even smaller money management firms and hedge funds now seek such entrée. Brokerage analysts, their research now less differentiated, are achieving more impact by arranging these meetings for the top clients, like a concierge. So the giant institutions and analysts are teaming up to book executive visits to the exclusion of small investors.

Some brokerages even judge their analyst performance partly based on their capability here. Brokerage in-house entities have been established to plan these meetings, field trips, tours, and engagements. According to Greenwich Associates, institutions indicate that some 26% of research commission fees are payments for "direct access to company management."

Corporate executives hold closed meetings with the buyside institutions. When Street sellside analysts accompany executives on a road show, they too are sometimes excluded from some of these sessions. Other investors are not admitted to these meetings. This is an extremely unbalanced degree of access and is conducive to inside tidbits, shadings, and extensive prescience from body language. Such gatherings are not webcast to all outside investors, or even broadcast on an open telephone conference call. They give the appearance of insider intimacy. The reality is that executives tend to communicate special insight to their most dominant institutional stockholders.

You'd be amazed at the advantage mega-institutional holders have in gaining contact with corporate management when sitting with a multi-million share position. Executive hearts pound at the thought of a 5% owner possibly dumping its position. A block of stock puts an institutional holder almost on par with a board member in terms of executive exposure and information flow. In comparison, Street analyst entrée is tantamount to that of the nighttime janitor. One-on-one confabs that big institutions have with management at analysts' conferences are closed. In fact, only the biggest-paying institutional clients gain this exclusive conference access. Big holders have inordinate influence over executives.

They also have advantageous social contact with executives. There are abundant opportunities at conferences, meetings, on the golf course, or over drinks for portfolio managers and even buyside analysts to glean, from corporate executives, key information on the stocks that they hold. As a sellside analyst, I pursued this avenue at places like the Los Angeles Country Club and the Turnberry golf resort in Scotland. It gave me an awareness superior to that gained in any formal encounters. Massive institutional stock positions act like alcohol—executives blab like guys at a bachelor party. Casual, collegial, social encounters between institutional investors (and, for that matter, sellside analysts) and corporate executives are rampant. Individual investors are not normally privy to these functions and once again are treated unfairly.

Overt influencing to achieve self-fulfilling stock price aims is a common occurrence on the buyside. Sometimes institutions communicate views conflicting with holdings. Institutions can verbally promote a stock that they are currently selling. Other times they offer bearish comments to drive a stock lower in order to purchase it cheaper. Hedge funds blast companies in which they hold a short position, a bet that the price will fall. Sellside analysts can no longer hold or communicate opinions opposite to their published recommendation. The buyside can still conduct such behavior.

Hedge Funds Distort Research and the Stock Market

There are more than 8,000 hedge funds controlling more than one trillion dollars in assets. The top 1,000 by assets are detailed in *Barron's* each week. Some two-thirds of all hedge funds are unregistered with the Securities Exchange Commission (SEC). The playing field is totally unfair. Brokers, money managers, mutual funds—almost all sides—must conform to SEC regulations. Not the hedgies, despite the new registration requirement. There is no full disclosure. Investment holdings do not have to be reported. There is little to inhibit the sometimes spreading of false rumors, misinformation, and spurious attacks. Hedge funds can essentially manipulate stocks in some cases to their own advantage. Short positions, can almost be a self-assuring process in the instances of unscrupulous campaigns where damaging statements and accusations are circulated. Such investment groups can selectively or serially dribble out disinformation or half truths. There is no requirement to disclose any deceptive story to outsiders all at the same time. Brokerage firms, mutual funds, even corporate executives are constrained from such methods, but not hedge funds.

The owners and managers of these entities, unlike mutual funds, keep for themselves some 20% of the annual investment gains. Thus, they tend to be extremely aggressive. They became powerful during the years of folly in the 1990s, adding a new dynamic to the market. Formerly unregulated, they soared into prominence, capital gains surging off the charts, and assets bulging. Universities, state pension funds, unions, and corporations earmarked a portion of their investments to this speculative, high-performance type of equity manager. The gains were too enticing to ignore, despite the risks. Because they are trade oriented, hedge funds generate enormous commissions for brokerage firms. They are in the top 10 list of biggest clients and are a high priority.

Many hedgies, assertive by nature, feel no hesitation in flexing their muscles. They can push analysts in inappropriate directions for their own purposes to unnaturally stimulate the funds' stock performance. Analysts may feel compelled to be cooperative in meeting their demands, realizing the importance of these monster commission-generating traders. Hedge funds sometimes coerce the Street into endorsing their positions, addressing and promulgating their stances, and occasionally trying to alter research views by passing along rumors or accusations. They can use the Street as a tool, passing self-serving stories on stocks that are often taken literally by salespeople and traders. Analysts must then react. If they vehemently disagree, they generate the ire of these lucrative clients. The stories sometimes have an air of believability, just enough to get the ear of analysts and investors. For the most part, though, such talk is embellished wishful thinking. It can be a lot of malarkey—propaganda to stimulate the prices of their trading positions.

Executives Rarely Think Their Company's Stock Price Is Excessive

Inexperienced analysts often fall prey to the cheering and puffery of corporate executives, easily interpreted by unproven analysts as confidence and an indication that business prospects appear glorious far into the future. Executives tend to take a Panglossian view of their outlook and try to suck analysts into this boosterism. Microsoft is a notable exception, and so was another stock I covered, Paychex. Its founder and chairman, Tom Golisano, pointedly referenced, during analyst conference calls, his trepidation amidst all the ecstasy of the late '90s Bubble Era that his smaller, loyal shareholders and employees would eventually get hurt once his stock valuation returned back to earth. He was correct. He knew the stratospheric level was unwarranted. But such an attitude is rare, and executives are seldom as forthright.

It's difficult to regulate against the corporate executive tendency to over-promote their stock. But this behavior is way overboard. On conference calls, managements spend 19 minutes accentuating the positives and 1 minute or no time at all on the negative issues, before opening the floor to Q & A. Some 99% of corporate press releases pertain to favorable news; the infrequent negative announcements are brief and hedged. TV interviews and analyst meetings are forums to push the bullish scenario. Most companies hold an annual one- or two-day analyst and institutional investor conference at their headquarters. The time they waste frustrating us with promotional marketing bullcrap drives us nuts. The positives are accentuated because the press is in attendance and the sessions are sometimes broadcast to the public. It's a PR show. Analysts have to attend, fearing we might miss some nuggets or inflections, but original, tangible, insightful content is miniscule. Any really useful information is extracted primarily from informal chats with executives during coffee breaks.

Corporate executives corrupt research analyst opinions, exerting extremely heavy coercion on analysts. A negative opinion creates an adverse reaction within the corporate ranks and the natural tendency is to retaliate. Analysts are punished. Our access to executives becomes limited. Phone calls are not returned, or are relegated to a low-level investor relations person. A bearish analyst is shunned when requesting a meeting, a form of being cut off. In conversations with institutional investors, CEOs lambaste analysts, disparaging them in order to discredit their unfavorable stock opinion. The behavior started in earnest during the 1990s euphoria. Executive efforts to drive their stock prices ever higher, like running up a one-sided football score, pushed analyst relations to the limit. Executives not only dangled investment banking business as a carrot for bullish investment ratings, they also used a stick to discourage negative opinions. Any stock rating other than complete exultation ruptured rapport with management, and the cold shoulder treatment ensued, topped off by bad-mouthing. Another subtle penalty meted out by executives for any analyst recommendation lacking total elation is relegation to the end of the line in the Q&A batting order on conference calls. Analysts always want to be early, if not first, to posture their clout to others listening in on the call.

I had established a credible record as the leading analyst in computer services and software, having been on Wall Street for more than two decades. The gregarious, glib, intense CEO of a company on which I carried a reserved opinion, was strident in his rather public castigation of my analytical abilities. His attack was launched to numerous institutional holders of the stock who filtered it back to me. He hoped they would bring pressure to bear on me to upgrade my recommendation. You can imagine my relationship with him and access to his fellow executives at the firm. Zilch. It diminished my respect for his team forever, even though, once I deemed it warranted, I eventually took a more upbeat stance on the stock.

Analysts must maintain friendly, collegial relationships with executives of the companies they cover in order to obtain a prompt and continuous flow of information. If we are cut off by executives, our research content is affected. We are unable to get favors such as the company's participation in a non-deal institutional client road show or to speak at our conferences. We need them, and they need us—an incestuous association. We must preserve our management sources, and a friendly association often has the deleterious effect of biasing our investment opinions.

There are a few exceptions, companies that are more even-handed, but such enlightened behavior is abnormal. I remember when the president of Automatic Data Processing, Frank Lautenberg, currently in his fourth term as U.S. Senator from New Jersey, wrote me a letter after I had downgraded my opinion on his stock. He communicated a magnanimous attitude of understanding and continuing open door access, instilling in me a feeling that I just couldn't wait for the time when I could appropriately upgrade it again. But that equitable approach is almost entirely out the window today.

Executives Curry Favor with Analysts to Prompt Favorable Opinions

Executives play favorites with analysts, which affects objectivity. And analysts are often too close to the management of the companies they cover. It is in the executives' interest to have their stocks rise so they push the Street to promote their companies' stocks. Their control over analysts is subtle, but effective. Executives give preferential treatment and access to analysts with bullish recommendations on the stock. Bullish analysts sponsor institutional client group field trips and are welcomed to meet with management at their headquarters, resulting in kudos and commissions. It's an influence that inhibits objective research.

An eBusiness Internet consulting company that I covered tried to appeal to my most basic desire. My investment opinion was lukewarm, actually skeptical, on this glorified webpage design firm. I didn't trust management, and the stock was wildly overvalued like all the other Internet names. The CEO sought to have me fall in line with all the exalted, biased, bullish investment opinions on his company. To curry my favor, knowing I was an avid golfer, he offered me the ultimate carrot: "Would you like to play at Augusta?" That's the quintessential Nirvana for anyone who plays the game. It's the home of the Masters, a "major" PGA tour event, and is extremely private and impenetrable. The enticement was tempting, but I boldly responded no. The thought of such an obvious inducement made me feel like barfing. And little did he know I had already kissed the hallowed grounds of Augusta on two occasions, my photo standing on Amen Corner already proudly displayed on my office wall.

Sometime after the bubble burst, an enthusiastic analyst was dismissed from his job when the National Association of Securities Dealers (NASD), the regulatory body, initiated charges over issuing misleading research reports and being too close to the management of a technology company he covered. In that tech company's legal proceedings, there was testimony that it spent $20,783 with an investigative service as a favor to the analyst in providing a background report on his fiancée. Nice trusting guy. The same analyst bestowed a $4,547 case of 1995 Chateau Margaux on the CEO, an unseemly gesture returned in kind with a $2,208 case of champagne. According to *The Wall Street Journal* coverage of a trial that the tech company was involved in, the analyst referred to himself in an email as a "LOYAL (company) EMPLOYEE." The NASD charged him with publishing reports on the firm lacking any mention of his own reservations. It fined the analyst $225,000 and suspended him for a year from the industry for providing "misleading and skewed research." An extreme case, but it illustrates the far-reaching influence of corporate executives on Street research.

There are numerous other corporate policies that disregard individual investors. These policies give preferential, unequal access to Street analysts. Executive inducement of analysts via selected entrée is a pernicious practice, but it's the norm. It is easy to blacklist analysts who carry negative investment ratings by affording preferential access to bullish analysts—that is, exclusive meetings with the CEO, invitations to user meetings, and headquarters visits with the analyst bringing along his select group of top clients. There is still a vacuum with respect to impartial, evenhanded executive access for all Street analysts. And if you think companies play favorites in terms of access with analysts, you can imagine where individuals stand in the pecking order regarding contact with management.

Corporations still tie their selection of an investment banking firm to research coverage and analyst opinions. It's amazing that executives continue to quietly seek favorable analyst coverage as a prerequisite to doing banking business with that brokerage firm. At a brokerage firm's pharmaceutical and biotechnology conference in early 2004, *The New York Times* reported a notable example of such a stance. In reaction to the analyst's required statement of his firm's investment banking intentions, the president of a biotech company was quoted as declaring with asperity, "The likelihood of an investment banking relationship is pretty close to zero until they upgrade their rating." The analyst's rating on the stock at the time was Neutral.

All these inherent factors distort the investment process. Don't be naive regarding the corruptive effect that not only the Street, but also institutional investors and corporate executives, have on individual investing. Street insiders are totally aware of these influences, and their investment decisions are not skewed by these detrimental practices.

3

Strategies in Quest of the Ideal Investment

Whenever I mention my professional background to people for the first time, they almost always react by asking me for investment advice. The expectation is that, as an insider, I can relate a nostrum for their haphazard investment endeavors that will put them on a sure track to stock market riches. After trying to change the subject, my normal response is to first inquire as to their goals, requirements, and financial situation. And the predictable reply I usually hear goes something like, "Well, my broker has put me in a bunch of stocks and mutual funds, and I have lost money in...." Individual investors sure need help, and it is not coming from Wall Street. Casual investors seem to believe that what they obtain from their brokers or Wall Street is reasonable investment advice—a big mistake. And they have no clue what to do on their own. This chapter lays out investment strategies and guidance so that you can *do it yourself*, which combined with an understanding of how the Street operates, should provide individuals with the tools to make smarter investment decisions.

Here are my time-tested, rational, conservative investment strategies that will serve as a basic investment foundation. I also lay out best stock market transaction practices. My last book, *Shakeout*, in 1984 offered 15 axioms "to protect the investor from the snares and pitfalls lurking behind every corner." Most are timeless: it never rains bad news, it pours; the first drop in profits is never the last; when insiders sell, you should too; beware of stock price fixation; the bigger their egos, the harder they fall; turnarounds are usually too little, too late; if you read it in the morning paper, it's too late; when management says things are bad, assume they are terrible; if you don't understand a company's business, management may not either, and the more likely a screw up will happen down the road; and new digs are a bad sign. This is an updated, vastly expanded version from the gut—strategies and practices that I believe must be an elemental underpinning for any investor.

Selecting the Best Company to Invest In

The first step in the process is the quest for the perfect company. Examining companies as prospective stock candidates is discussed in detail in Chapter 4, "Evaluating Companies as Investment Candidates." As a starter, here are a few simple characteristics to look for that are key to any quality investment.

Find Unique, Focused Companies Leading a New or Niche Market

The ideal investment is a company that is unique in some manner, a leader in an emerging market or technology, dominant in an attractive niche sector, or somehow different. The distinctiveness might be in the strategy it takes within an established market. The key is focus and expertise that is unusual, that sets the company apart; a structural characteristic that allows robust, dependable profit generation. This is the "story" aspect, why the company is dissimilar to peer group competitors. I avoid the me too, second- or third-largest players in a sector unless they are taking an atypical tact that makes them better. It is this element of singularity that I assess first when considering an equity investment.

Look for Specialized, Simple Businesses

Firms *specializing* in a focused product area, market, or approach, like JetBlue, Starbucks, or eBay, always outrun the generalists. Specialists have notable advantages over bigger, broader lumbering giants. They are nimble, aggressive, concentrated, and emerging. Like in a PGA tour golf tournament on Sunday, it's easier to come from behind than defensively protect a lead. Invest in *simple* businesses that are readily understandable, rather than complex areas like high tech and biotech that necessitate extreme expertise to judge the merits or appraise the outlook. This is the Warren Buffet style.

Seek Double-Digit Growth or Robust Cash Generation

The ultimate indicator of steady expansion is revenue, not profits. Growth companies should be achieving double-digit revenue gains on a consistent basis with no funny stuff like unbilled revenue or unusual, unsustainable big upfront contract deals. I want to see *real* growth that is repeatable going forward. But nothing excessive. Expansion rates of over 25% cannot be maintained over an extended period, and you are probably paying for the current exorbitant pace in the form of a high price/earnings multiple. Companies can readily manipulate earnings by cutting costs, accounting treatment, reserves, restructuring, stock buybacks, and any number of measures. Profit improvement can be achieved with mirrors for quite a while. Revenue is the true test. There are myriad cases, like IBM, where profits have expanded for years but with little revenue growth. This indicates maturity in the business. I need to see evidence of vibrant growth prospects. Favorable cash flow is always important. Negative cash flow is a red flag. Sometimes if growth is not the objective, then highly positive cash flow is imperative. If investment is for dividend yield returns, then cash flow is king.

Pursue Healthy, Stable, or Expanding Profit Margins

This is another measure of corporate vigor. It's not the absolute level of operating margins or pretax profit margins (that varies by industry); it's the overall pattern during the last few years that counts. I prefer profit margins at the higher end of the peer group norm, indicating either good management or a unique business approach. More importantly, margins must be steady, with no pattern of erosion or slippage. Some improvement is the ideal. The combination of revenue growth plus profit margin expansion is a powerful favorable earnings impetus. But watch out for companies where profit margins are so far superior to any other industry competitors that there may be no more room to widen—that is, where margins might be maxed out and possibly at risk.

Insist on a Robust Balance Sheet and Quality Finances

Companies with high levels of debt are risky. I prefer no long-term debt and minimal short-term debt. The debt to capitalization ratio should be under 20%. Other balance sheet items should also be superior, with accounts receivable turnover under 90 days, no unbilled revenue, and nothing complex or out of alignment. Read the footnotes to understand the rationale behind things like deferred revenue, capitalized software, depreciation/amortization, and capital spending. On the quarterly conference call, you'll hear if such balance sheet items disturb the analysts, which is a caution flag. The simpler the better; multiple pages of extensive footnotes in quarterly and annual reports or SEC filings bother me.

Look for All-Around Quality in Executives, Customers, Board Members, and Partners

Seek and stick with quality companies. The first step is to consider the company they keep. Are the customers blue chip entities? Is there an ongoing year after year relationship with these major clients? I want to see the best accounting firms, commercial bankers, investment bankers, securities analysts, board members, law firms, and joint venture partners associated with any firm that I'm considering as an investment. Excellence also pertains to executives, employees, products, and services, even to the major institutional investor holders of the stock. What is the background of management? Where was their past experience; did they work at winning companies? High-class companies understate earnings by an average of 5%, while low-caliber firms overstate their profits by 10%–15%. Not surprising—it's just like the character of people. Looking at companies is like assessing a new home, automobile, job, or spouse; you want quality to the greatest degree possible.

Avoid Arrogant, Overconfident Management

Corporate executives who have an egotistical and arrogant attitude make for a high-risk investment. They usually have a blind side and are set up for a fall. Overconfidence is a killer. Look for management that is humble, understated, and conservative, with a sense of humor. It is fine for them to be aggressive, enthusiastic, with belief in their mission. But I like to see humility as embodied by Harry S. Truman during the 1944 Democratic Convention. He was informed by President Roosevelt, who because of ill health was unlikely to serve out his next term, that he would be the vice presidential candidate. His reply, "Oh shit!" Not that I want corporate executives to banter abundant expletives, but I prefer executives with an unassuming nature.

Prefer Smaller Companies Over Giants

Small and mid-sized firms can still be specialists, are able to stay focused, and are manageable. New thrusts and strategies have an impact. Small companies are capable of changing directions quickly and more swiftly attacking the competition. It's easier for good management to be creative and original, to make a small-sized company distinctive. Companies under $1–$2 billion in revenue can sustain vigorous growth and attract better employees. They are sizeable enough to have financial strength and stability but are still on the make, seeking to achieve industry leadership. Such companies have less Street research coverage, and are less owned by institutions, so their stocks may not be excessively exploited or overbought.

Avoid Weird Stock Structures or Sweetheart Management Setups

I dislike companies that have two classes of stock: one for the founder giving him all the voting power, and another for outsiders with little effective governing powers. Google is a case in point, with dual-class voting stocks, one for the founders/management and the other for public shareholders. This obviates management and insider accountability to shareholders. Phantom shares are similarly suspect, where stockholders do not own the assets but only a vague right to dividends. Sometimes classes of stock are created as an anti-takeover device, to artificially protect management. Look for other vested interests management deals that indicate parochial behavior, such as close friends or pliable supporters on the board. I am leery of stock appreciation rights, reissuance of stock options at lower levels after a stock price nose dive, and other lucrative, sweetheart management arrangements. Needless to say, I view backdating of stock options unkindly, as almost corrupt, speaking volumes about management principles. I abhor the disproportionate management compensation so prevalent these days. Be careful of managements that have too many perks, such as preferred parking slots, company drivers, corporate aircraft, sumptuous headquarters, sports arena courtesy suites, or names on stadiums and ballparks (Enron Field comes to mind).

Investment Strategies Must Start With Capital Preservation

Next are some key investment strategies for you to follow—simple and straightforward, but surprisingly often overlooked. I present them in approximate order of importance. As an individual investor, you have the flexibility to use these suggestions and take advantage of your position in contrast to the constraints on institutional portfolio managers.

Preserving Capital Is the First Priority

Protection of capital is paramount, an investment objective far ahead of gains and returns. If you doubt me, just ask anyone who watched their nest egg, even their home equity loans, melt to zilch as the 1990s bubble burst. The magnitude of gains is almost irrelevant compared to the preservation of your investment pool. It's just too difficult to replace. After a 50% drop in a stock, it requires a 100% rise in the price to get back to even. Like the veracity of an analyst Buy recommendation, there is little issue whether it rises 10% or 50%, but it's a major disaster if it declines 30%. So always be conservative, think in terms of downside potential and risk. Be cognizant that highly improbable "Black Swan" events having extreme impact occur from time to time, as pointed out in *Black Swan*, a book by Nassim Taleb. Have the discipline to take modest losses, say 10%–15%, before they become a serious debacle, a drop of more than 25%. You are a hero, or actually a wealthy person, if you just maintain your investment capital and perhaps achieve 5%–10% appreciation annually for 30 years. In conjunction with this, you need to have low expectations. Don't assume audacious future returns because that will veer you away from your foremost objective of preserving capital. A *Financial Analysts Journal* article by Asness summarizes my feelings precisely: "In true Hippocratic fashion, Do No Harm!"

The point here is *don't lose*; avoid incurring whopping losses. That is the secret of superior investing. Charles D. Ellis makes the point in another *Financial Analysts Journal* article that "large losses are forever—in investing, teenage driving, and fidelity...and are almost always caused by trying to get too much by taking too much risk." He discusses the excitement of "the big score," with too much emphasis on offense, little regard to defense. Laurence D. Fink, CEO of BlackRock, quips that "the pain of losing money is far greater than the glory of making money." Another mutual fund, the T. Rowe Capital Appreciation Fund, also illustrates the point. It has achieved a gain every single year of its existence, 16 years in a row. That includes the 3 years when the market declined, 2000–2002. It does not attempt to maximize its upside but rather minimize the downside to protect capital. The attitude expressed by its fund managers, according to an article in the *Wall Street Journal*, is "How much can we lose if we're wrong?" You are already taking enough risk by owning common stocks and even more so by holding only a few names; thus, a conservative approach is warranted. Good investment results depend on not losing.

Invest in Themes and Rising Industry Sectors

The way to be stunningly correct and take long rides on stellar performers is to be early in an industry sector that is breaking out for fundamental reasons. Identify an area where fundamentals are shifting for the better or where circumstances should be improving over the next year or so. Real estate and REITs were superb as interest rates dropped in 2003–2004 and as real estate prices climbed in 2005; the energy sector—oil and gas—took off in 2004 because of war and shortages, an economic upswing, China demand, disruptions, and world political uncertainty, and continued in 2005–2007; precious metals and commodities were a robust area in 2005–2007. Technology was the target of overinvestment for more than a decade; it's over-capitalized, with too many venture capital firms shoving billions at the sector. Energy is under-capitalized; amazingly, there is too little investment capital. Real estate is now over-capitalized, with REITs and other investors having plowed in zillions there. Stick with sectors that are still underinvested, underexploited. It's not too late to invest in a few different stocks in a sector that is already starting to accelerate, there is typically a long ramp. And you don't have to be a fortune teller to figure out the emerging new theme. But be cautious of trends. Sometimes they may be narrower, more mature, or already fully exploited by investors by the time you recognize them, say Starbucks, Whole Foods, and Amazon. Look for broad themes rather than trendy ideas. Pay attention, read, observe, and think.

A particularly easy method by which to participate in an industry sector is through exchange traded funds (ETFs). There are many such funds now representing everything from the S&P 500, to financial stocks, to gold. They are a pure play in the segment, holding a fixed number of representative stocks. In the case of commodities, they own the actual material, like crude oil or gold. They are actively traded, listed on the major exchanges, and are simple. You can own a precise, narrow grouping within the market without buying five or ten individual stocks on your own. If you like the health/biotech industry as a theme, you can buy that ETF, or the insurance sector, or tech, oil, silver, precious metals, or how about Japanese stocks, short-term U.S. Treasuries, utilities, telecom, natural resources, European stocks, the emerging market, or even the entire international market excluding the U.S. There are even ETFs focused on ignored stocks with little or no analyst coverage, and stocks reflecting favorable corporate insider buying and Wall Street analyst upgrades.

A drawback is that if the ETF owns the actual commodity, so do you. Gains are taxed as collectibles, at a maximum of 28%, rather than a 15% long-term capital gains tax if the ETF comprises stocks. Another caveat is that investors might start to think they are consistently proficient in choosing the right sector at the right time (sector timing), and this can become a form of trading. Don't get into a syndrome of flipping ETFs every few months. They should be viewed as investment vehicles. And there are no dividends. So don't go crazy.

Hold Only a Modest Number of Stocks and Choose Familiar Companies

I suggest owning no more than five or ten different stocks. Too many breeds ignorance. A casual friend sitting next to me at a black tie dinner who fancied himself an avid investor boasted that he held 300 different equities! After gagging on my salmon, I inquired if he was a portfolio manager of the Magellan Fund, which probably doesn't hold anywhere near as many positions. My argument against broad diversification is that an array of so-called alternative investments, like gold, commodities, and emerging market stocks, offer little protection in a falling market. World financial markets are so interlinked now that diversification isn't what it used to be. On the day of the more than 400-point market drop in February 2007, the China and European markets also plummeted, as did corporate bond prices, oil, and even gold.

Peter Lynch refers to owning too many stocks as "de-worseification." A survey by the universities of Michigan and Illinois agrees with me, finding that investors with only a handful of names outperformed more diversified portfolios. Investors holding numerous stocks slightly lagged the markets. It has to do with knowledge, familiarity, and information. The fewer the companies, the greater the understanding. Local firms are even better, an investor is likely to know more about these businesses and have more thorough intelligence. And smaller stocks, less well-known, according to the survey, outperform the S&P 500 Index in these concentrated portfolios.

Low Price/Earnings Multiples Reduce Risk

I prefer stocks that carry lower PE multiples than the norm of companies in their sector. This provides more opportunity for multiple expansion and tends to reduce volatility. There is less downside when bad news surfaces. High PE multiple stocks hit a massive vacuum if there is even a slight earnings disappointment, a double whammy—sharp earnings estimate reduction and major multiple contraction. Modest PEs leave less room for a major stock price collapse. The stellar stocks over time have always started out with reasonable valuations. Even fabulous companies with brilliant prospects can be poor investments if your entry price is too high. John B. Neff, who was a renowned manager of value mutual funds at the Vanguard Group for 31 years, said it all in a CFA Institute Financial Analysts Seminar in mid-2006, "Having a low P/E is the primary principal."

To illustrate the merit of modest PEs, each year a Bloomberg columnist identifies the 10 U.S. stocks with the lowest PEs out of all those over $500 million in market cap. For several years in a row, they way outperformed the S&P 500. That same major brokerage finding referred to earlier in the discussion of under-followed stocks, as indicated in *Barron's*, revealed that the second best out of 20 investment strategies in 2006 was to hold stocks that had low PE multiples. Various other studies have also shown that high PE multiple stocks yield low returns to investors compared to low PE stocks.

Dividend Yield Is Important

During the bubble years, dividends were neglected; companies paying them were considered dodo birds. Yield is now back in vogue. Historically, from 1926–2006, the total stock market return averaged close to 11% annually, and 41% of this, or 4.4% of the gain each year, stemmed from dividends according to the Motley Fool Income Investor. They may play an even more important role in the future if the market gains ease to 5%–8%. Dividend yield is a key indicator of financial stability, good cash flow, and quality. And a dividend provides some downside protection during a setback. A $20 stock that pays an $0.80 dividend, a 4% yield, is unlikely to plummet to $8, indicating a 10% yield, unless the firm is about to slash the dividend payout. The downside is more likely $10–$15; that is, a 5%–8% yield—the dividend, if safe, providing an effective floor.

There are studies such as the one by Robert D. Arnott, editor of the *Financial Analysts Journal*, and Asness that show a direct positive correlation between dividend payout ratios and earnings growth. The higher the payout, the faster the earnings pace. This startling relationship probably indicates that managements paying out higher dividends have confidence in bright future earnings growth prospects. Dividends also reduce excess cash on hand, forcing executives to be careful and make wiser decisions in picking investment projects. It's my view that in the future, companies will be distributing more of their earnings in the form of dividends. Payout ratios will rise. There's no reason for companies not to pay out 50% of their profits. But many managements are afraid that investors may misinterpret this as a signal of maturity and inability to reinvest in the growth of the business, so they hoard their cash and it drags down returns.

Hold Stocks Long-Term

This means at least one year, preferably several years. The best performance is invariably with stocks that prove to be winners over 5–10 years. Perfect timing in entry price and capturing the top price tick on the sale is virtually impossible, especially on a trading basis over the short-term. Such factors are minimized if you are investing rather than trading, to say nothing of lower capital gains taxes and fewer commissions. It's a long distance race requiring self-discipline and patience. There have been numerous studies proving that a long range buy-and-hold strategy reduces risk. According to Burton G. Malkiel, Professor of Economics at Princeton University and author of *A Random Walk Down Wall Street,* in any given 1-year or 5-year period, the market return historically has ranged from a 25%–50% gain to a decline of 25%. But in virtually any 15-year span, the annual market return has always been ahead by some 5%–20%. A study by Ilia Dichev, a professor at the University of Michigan, detailed in *The American Economic Review,* reveals a 10% average return for investors who bought and held listed securities from 1926–2002. If trading, the return was 8.6%. And if buying-and-holding NASDAQ stocks from 1973–2002, the average annual return was 9.6% versus 4.3% for the typical trader.

During most of my career, I made client marketing treks to Europe on a regular 18-month basis. On these trips to meet with institutions, I observed a practice that can be valuable to you as an individual investor. European institutional investors allocate a portion of their portfolios to U.S. stocks, and they bring a refreshingly more rational investment philosophy compared with the U.S. trading mentality. I found that Europeans followed a longer-term investment strategy and *invested* in U.S. stocks over the *long-term.* U.S. investors should take a hint from Europe. Be an investor, not a trader. The distance, time difference (NYSE trading begins at 2:30 PM in Paris), and less contact with U.S. company executives and analysts may be the reason. They are not as absorbed by quarterly portfolio performance.

Trading Is Entertaining, But Like Gambling, It's Usually Fruitless

Short-term trading is highly challenging even for veterans on broker-age trading floors, who are in instant contact on all rumors, opinion shifts, news, and other influences that have an immediate impact on stock prices. If you think you're smart enough to achieve consistent gains by furious buying and selling, you're probably also telling your friends you always win at the tables in Vegas. A relatively tiny portion of your portfolio should be earmarked for trading, maybe 5%–10% maximum, if you are so bored that you need such thrills and spills in your life. Maybe once you lose that 5% of your assets, you will be cured of the addiction. And don't think holding stocks for a few months isn't trading. Trying to make money by buying and selling stocks during a several-month span is a fool's game. In *Barron's* January 2006 Roundtable, 12 leading, well-known money managers in the country made 85 specific recommendations. Slightly more than 5 months later, 41 of these picks, almost half, proved faulty and had gone in the wrong direction. And these were the experts, the insiders. So, be an investor—trading is a gamble.

Wall Street just keeps getting ever more short-term oriented. So do CNBC and other media sources. They constantly promote quick-paced trading, in and out, generating transactions and commissions for brokers and continuous reliance on the media. James Cramer on CNBC actually treats investing (this style is really trading) as a game. Street recommendations are almost never aimed at more than a 1-year timeframe. The average length New York Stock Exchange stocks were held in 2006 was under 7 months, according to Sanford Bernstein. This compares to over 12 months back in 1999, itself the epitome of the day-trading era. You need to avoid this temptation, and not get caught up in the sizzle or gambling-like aspect of trading. It's a losing game. You can outperform the Street by steering clear of that frenzy. That's their game. Play your game.

NYSE-Listed Stocks Preferred Over NASDAQ Shares

I suggest that almost all of the names in a portfolio should be NYSE companies. The listing requirements of the New York Stock Exchange are more rigorous than NASDAQ, another screen providing an improved measure of quality and stability. The pool of NYSE listings carries, on balance, lower PEs, better dividends, and higher quality, though there are notable exceptions like Microsoft and Intel, both stalwart NASDAQ names. NYSE stocks are more actively traded and get more attention from the press. Only a tiny portion of a personal portfolio, no more than 10%, should be devoted to aggressive, speculative equities, more prevalent on the NASDAQ. If you are trading rather than investing, NASDAQ names may be more appropriate.

Tread Lightly with International Companies

U.S. companies entail less risk for investors and are easier to follow than international firms. Foreign entities have different accounting, securities regulations, and are subject to foreign currency fluctuations and a myriad of other factors that complicate the picture. If a Japanese stock rises 25% in yen value but the currency there declines 25% relative to the U.S. dollar, an American investor breaks even, with no gain in dollar terms. Even if the shares are listed on the NYSE or have ADRs (American depository receipt) traded in the U.S., it's still a dice roll. Try to scrutinize the financial statements of a German or Brazilian company. Forget about it. The only exception may be Canadian equities, though there still could be foreign currency perils. It's a challenge to get it right with a U.S. stock; once you go abroad, it becomes almost a shot in the dark. If you insist on owning an international company, be sure it is listed on the NYSE, it follows FASB accounting rules, management speaks in English on conference calls, and Wall Street publishes reports and earnings estimates—in other words, a quasi-U.S. type of company that you can readily analyze and track. Maybe you think Chinese or European stocks will be a robust investment area, or forecast that the U.S. dollar will be weak and want to benefit from stronger foreign currencies. A lower risk method of participating in international markets is by investing in an ETF comprised of international stocks.

Turnarounds Almost Never Work

Often turnarounds are merely milking the operation for cash flow to return to investors, usually in the form of stock buybacks, a financial means to inflate earnings per share. It's all a mirage. A company crashes, revenue and earnings nose dive, new competitors come along trashing the old guard, and finally the board replaces management with a promising new team. All of a sudden the outlook is bright, pregnant with renewal prospects. Don't fall for it. Restructuring, divestitures, write-offs, new directions, fresh strategies, and different management— it's a temporary game. The stock rises on the illusion of a turnaround. But real revenue growth and sustained improvement in operating earnings rarely happen. A lower cost structure, less debt burden, and financial re-engineering boost profits only momentarily. These are mirrors. Real orders, contracts, demand, and growth are almost impossible to reestablish once a company has run off the railroad tracks. The IBM story over the last decade has involved negligible internal revenue growth, but rather foreign currency gains, acquisitions and divestitures, write offs, and stock buybacks. A turnaround is a trading opportunity at best, and is never a long-term investment.

Don't Try to Catch a Falling Safe

You might think a stock is cheap after its price has been sliced to a fraction of its former high. It's not. The stock almost always continues to descend. Remember how many Internet dot.com wonders that hit triple figures seemed cheap when they got to $10? Most went on to $1 or 0. Street analysts make the same mistake all the time. The first bad news is never the last. In spring 2007, the sub-prime mortgage lending firms were imploding. A *New York Times* story referred to a Bear Stearns analyst who upgraded one such company, whose stock had been axed in 3 weeks by 50% to about $15. The familiar refrain was that downside risk was limited at that point. A couple of weeks later, the shares were selling for less than $1. In the '90s Bubble Era, I resisted the urge to chase Internet and other high-tech stocks that were surging to the moon, which saved me a bundle once the bubble burst. My capital was protected. If the basic fundamentals do not warrant some ridiculous valuation, take a pass. Don't position yourself under a falling safe, thinking you can catch it. You'll get flattened.

Of course, there are times when being a contrarian investor is a brilliant strategy. I remember that October day in 1987 when the stock market crashed 22%. I purchased some shares of one of the best computer services stocks I was covering, and it was a lucrative investment decision. Eight months later, the market had recovered. If a company's prospects are solid and its stock is being given away, go for it.

Avoid Participating in Initial Public Offerings (IPOs)

Obtaining a few shares of an IPO is a fool's game. As an individual investor, you will never be allocated any shares in a hot new offering anyway. Brokerage firms direct the best deals almost exclusively to their biggest-paying clients, the institutions. Only the new issues that cannot attract enough institutional interest tend to be made available to individual retail clients. And those are precisely the stocks you don't need to own. Even if you are able to wrangle a few shares of an attractive IPO, the initial pricing is usually no particular bargain. Buying shares a few days after a company becomes publicly traded is even worse; the hype and support is at its peak. Investment banking firms ballyhoo the story before the offering, there is artificial propping of the price for a period after the offering, and invariably thirty days later, the analyst comes out with a positive investment rating. But then the euphoria starts to subside. Six months after the issuance the management lock-up period expires, and they become eligible to sell their insider shares, adding an overhang pressure. At this stage, it's back to business as usual but gravity sets in and the shares have to sink or swim without contrived support. The bottom line is that the track record of IPOs is lackluster, with the tendency being to underperform the market.

Mutual Funds Are No Panacea; the Cost of Safety Is Boring Mediocrity

I avoid mutual funds. Most of them underperform the market. From 1983 to 2003, the S&P 500 return averaged 13.0% annually, easily exceeding the 10.3% average return from equity mutual funds. They are so diversified, it is difficult to achieve exceptional gains above the indexes. Some have upfront or exit fees, all have management fees, and there are tax considerations. The average mutual fund expense ratio is now 1.6%, in excess of the commission you pay on a stock transaction. Mutual funds are okay if you choose to totally outsource your investments, but if so, why are you reading this book? Sure...balance, a wide assortment of securities, and professional management at mutual funds all lend a measure of conservative protection. And it's unlikely you will suddenly lose 50% of your capital. But the price of this safety net is boring mediocrity. If you just want to be a stock market participant, go with index funds or ETFs that track precisely and mechanically a given stock market or industry sector, and don't bother reading the rest of this book.

Mutual funds hold stocks an average of 11 months and are therefore short-term traders. They have high portfolio turnover and are necessarily aggressive due to quarterly performance measurements. So it's heavy offense and little defense. Individuals can act differently and avoid such speculative behavior. Funds tend to rent a stock; you can own a stock. I suggest managing your own personal mutual fund of 5–10 stocks. That's enough concentration in individual securities so each holding can make a meaningful impact. It's an adequate array to avoid having all your eggs in one basket. And it provides the exhilaration of putting your own stamp on your own portfolio. Using this approach, individuals have a superior prospect of outperforming compared to big-time mutual fund portfolio managers who are burdened with constraints.

Disregard Brokerage Recommended or Emphasis Lists

These preferred stock recommendation lists published by most brokerage firms state the obvious. The names are already in favor and the stocks are up in price, no longer representing good value. They are broadly held and well discovered, so it's just too late. As discussed earlier, brokerage approval committees are like lemmings. If the stock is depressed and has lagged, it will not be added to the list because it appears wimpy on the charts. If it's a good story and the share price has shown nice progress, it's easy for them to shove it onto their best idea index. To an individual investor, these lists may signify stocks that probably should continue to be held if already owned but they are certainly not original, astute investment proposals. Once a stock is on the list, though, there is only one way to go; that's the eventual yanking off, often times on a whim, which propels the stock price lower.

Flag Your Purchase Date; Focus on the One-Year Mark

Be aware of the date when a stock investment passes the one-year holding period, when the reduced 15% federal long-term capital gains tax rate kicks in. Once a stock has been owned for a year, it's easier to take a long-term view and ascertain whether the original investment thesis is proving to be correct. I have been embarrassed a few times when for compelling reasons I've—stupidly—pulled the trigger on a sale a mere week or two before the holding period went long-term; that is, one year. I should never have sacrificed the bargain 15% tax rate.

Short-Term Trading Positions Should Be Contracted

Once in a while, there may be a short-term trading opportunity, say when a stock has plummeted on an overreaction to negative news and a "dead cat bounce" or rebound is expected; or, when there seems imminently favorable news or you anticipate a forthcoming negative event. If it's a *trade*, stick to the short-term plan, eliminate the position within a limited timeframe regardless of whether the idea was a winner or a non-event. Do not let the stock sit around and clutter up your portfolio with a modest gain or little performance. Don't be pacified or lulled beyond a short couple months span if it's a trading position.

Pragmatic Investing Practices and Techniques

After you have a grasp of appropriate investment strategies, there are some pragmatic investing practices that I recommend. These are the mechanics that should help optimize results and prevent emotional reactions that can cause the wrong transaction decision. It's like football. After establishing a winning game plan, each individual play must be executed. So now it's a matter of technique.

Once You Decide, Take Action

Once you have finally determined an investment choice, after researching, analyzing, pondering, and considering...pull the trigger.

Don't sit around and hesitate. Make the move. And don't quibble over pennies per share in price. Limit orders are appropriate when the stock is not actively traded so you won't get screwed like a typical retail client. But don't try to low-ball a purchase price or be too greedy on a sell. Your order might not get completed. Implementation is even more critical on the sale. Trust your conclusion. Have confidence in your decision. And don't waste time in the exit action. There is nothing more exasperating than making the correct investment decision and not benefiting because you have procrastinated or messed up the simple process of concluding the transaction.

Avoid Selling the Day of a Dramatic Downgrade

Most of the damage to a stock has already happened within an hour or so after a summary drop in an investment opinion by a brokerage analyst. Don't get caught up in the emotional rush to the door. There is invariably a bounce back the next day or within a week or so. Hold your fire for a better-selling opportunity once the dust settles. And you probably should not sell in any case. Don't do what Wall Street says. The same for a striking opinion upgrade. Wait a day or two for the excitement to abate and the stock to back off. And this holds true for stocks that are added or deleted from brokerage recommended lists. Delay any transaction until the initial influence wanes.

Most Downgrades Are Late;
The Stock Price has Already Fallen

The first Street downgrade on a stock may be a fair indication that the shares are headed lower on forthcoming negative problems. And that initial call is your best, if not only, chance to sell. But even then the stock is usually already way below its high. Most opinion reductions are "me too," the fourth or fifth such recommendation alterations on the Street, all copycats once the dismal outlook is already highly evident. The shares have usually fallen 25%–50% or more, already troughed, and have fully discounted the plethora of bad news. The bulk of downgrades is late and represents the final capitulation. Often this represents a good buying entry point for a patient value investor. Once most Street analysts are pessimistic, the share price has only one way to go—back up.

Don't Buy or Sell in Reaction to Press Articles or Media Information

Once it appears in the newspaper, magazines, on TV, or in the general media, the information has already impacted the stock price. The story probably raced around Wall Street the day before or even weeks ago. And you are too emotional, irrational, and reactive. Wait a couple of days for things to settle down, so you can make a more dispassionate decision, after you've had time to balance all the factors. There's an old saw about investing that bears repeating, "buy on rumor, sell on news." I mention it because most individual investors do the opposite. Press stories should be used to gain in-depth background information, a more thorough understanding of a company and its prospects. Although the media may give you insight on sectors, trends, markets, areas in which you might consider investments, and long-term stock investment ideas, stories that appear on stocks are already common knowledge to most Wall Street insiders. It's good to be aware of what others are thinking—for example, that a company may go bankrupt or new bookings are slipping in a certain industry; just don't think you have any unique, early insight stemming from media news. Don't think it's actionable. Once the story is on a magazine cover, it has been analyzed and researched by the author for awhile. It might be news to you, but it's already reflected in the stock price. A *Financial Analysts Journal* study by professors Arnot, Earl Jr., and North at the University of Richmond showed that favorable cover articles occurred after a period of positive results and the opposite for negative cover stories. In fact, once these cover stories were published, the news was about to reverse, according to the findings.

Pay Attention to Contrary Evidence

Once you have made an investment commitment, there is a tendency to focus heavily on favorable support that bolsters your decision. Human nature pushes you to disregard any contrary, negative input that could prove you wrong. The trap is to fall in love with your viewpoint, always seeking evidence to fortify your position. You must be brutally objective, skeptical, and questioning. Even if you are correct initially, things change over time and circumstances may necessitate rethinking the original stance at some juncture. Keep an open mind.

Constantly probe for the counter, negative developments. Be wary by nature. And similarly, in the reverse. If you have avoided a stock because of a gloomy view, there may be a point where it's appropriate to take a more positive attitude.

Clean Up Your Portfolio and Rethink Your Strategy Periodically

The best occasions to review your investments are at year end or during vacations. Rethink your overall strategy or themes and shake off any emotional paralysis that has locked you into certain stock positions. A market analyst I respect, Ray DeVoe, Jr., terms this "liberation from the prison of past decisions." Some stocks may have attained too heavy a weighting for your peace of mind. However, this is where I disagree with most "experts," those who advise periodic rebalancing by trimming back oversized positions. Your biggest winners that become the outsized positions in your portfolio are probably the last thing you should contemplate selling. I prefer a higher weighting in my best investments rather than just a normal position. If you believe that the prospect remains favorable for one of your most sizeable stock positions, buy more, if anything, rather than cutting it back.

Other stocks you own may have lagged for so long, it's time to give up. What is your comfort level or enthusiasm with each individual stock in your portfolio? Maybe your theme is stale; are there newly emerging trends to begin investing in? There are tax considerations when taking gains; maybe there are losers to be used as an offset. A reticence to sell stocks that haven't worked out—that is, to admit past mistakes—is normal. But by not selling your losers and moving on, you commit another mistake. Accept your failures, step up to the plate, and dump your junk so you can start afresh. It only hurts for a bit, and then you feel liberated. I won't make any analogies here.

I think distance or a relaxing change of venue like a beach resort, when you are not inundated by everyday distractions, is a perfect opportunity to ponder your holdings. Take your monthly brokerage statement and mull it over at the pool with your piña colada. I do this a couple of times a year. The more rum punches, the better my investment strategies...well, kind of. One footnote here. If you have been away and out of touch with the stock market, financial news, and the price changes in your holdings, don't pull the trigger on any portfolio transactions on your first day back. First get up to speed and familiarize yourself with any investment news that you missed. Reassessment and review in a disciplined manner is especially critical in December in order to make year-end investment changes that have tax implications.

Be Alert to the January Effect

Yes investors, there is a January effect. That is, as January goes, so goes the whole year. There does not seem to be any logical, or broadly accepted reason. So don't try to analyze it. The facts are, as found by professors Cooper, McConnell, and Outchinnikov laid out in the *CFA Digest*, that if the market return is up in January, then the average gain is 14.8% over the remaining 11 months. When the stock market drops in the first month of the year, the average return is just 2.9% during the rest of the year. This was the case from 1940–2003. Watch January closely for clues to the year ahead.

Exchange Ideas with Informed Associates

Seek out like-minded investors, not traders, who have a degree of investment maturity, experience, and knowledge. Exchange opinions and views with these associates about the market, industry trends, investment ideas, and other stock-related insight. Don't accept their commentary blindly, though; use it as a source to further investigate and research. Ponder the information, the qualifications and reliability of the purveyor, and any vested interest of the proponent. Take advantage of your professional, informed contacts, a friend of a friend who is a member of management, ideas from golfing partners and old high school buddies. But always balance such input. The best fertilization comes from ongoing relationships where there is consistent contact, not one-shot run-ins.

Beware of Amateurs Recommending Their Stocks; They Love Reinforcement

You will rarely get an objective stock idea from friends that are rank amateur investors. They are in love with the stocks they own and are partial. If you take their recommendations, it reinforces their picks, makes them feel better, and gives them a sense of power or influence. This is dangerous. It's personal. Friends feel vindicated and their portfolio selections justified when others play copycat. It's a natural human tendency. Always research any such ideas yourself before acting on them. A friend can be a highly subjective research source, so be skeptical.

Read the Wall Street Journal, *Be Aware, and Stay Abreast of Trends*

This is background knowledge. By perusing the *Wall Street Journal* or *Investor's Business Daily*, the *New York Times* business section, and *Barron's*, you can keep up with current investment strategies, changes/shifts, sector trends and ideas, and the bigger picture. The same for TV investment programs, such as Bloomberg, CNBC, or Lou Dobbs. These media sources are good for perspective on equities, bonds, real estate, treasuries, commodities, options, annuities, and all types of investments. But don't get too bogged down in details or specific investment recommendations.

Little of Essence Is Revealed in Quarterly Earnings Press Releases

When a company's quarterly earnings appear on the newswire don't expect to learn much. Quarterly reports are of relatively little value, mostly puff pieces or watered-down commentary. The numbers are far from the real truth of what is occurring in the business. Reported results are superficial. Street analysts figure out the real meaning within a few minutes, hop on their firms' squawk boxes, and the substance of this progress report is immediately reflected in the stock price. You can interpret the results by looking at the stock price. Don't feel that you have to instantly jump on the press release. Scan it leisurely later. Listen in on the company conference call (open to the public) to ascertain a more complete picture of a company's quarter and its current outlook.

Listen to Your Companies' Quarterly Earnings Conference Calls

Conference calls are publicized ahead of time on the company's website and can be dialed into, or the webcast can be viewed via the Internet. The replay is usually available for a few days after the live broadcast. Pay attention to the management tone, discern whether they sound trustworthy. Become familiar with the business and operations. Are executives humble, focused, detailed, and objective or are they are full of hype and BS? Are the Wall Street analysts' questions negatively couched or neutral? This is as close to getting an inside look as you'll ever have. It's a fabulous one-hour investment of time. Once you've heard a few of these, you'll get a sense as to your comfort level or whether the executives make you uneasy. It's far better than reading boring, unoriginal, tedious research reports and filings. It's the difference between reading a biography and sitting down to chat in-depth with the actual person. Conference calls are examined further in Chapter 6, "How Street Analysts Really Operate."

Executive Briefings and Analyst Meetings Usually Send Stocks Lower

Annual all-day analyst meetings at headquarters or major New York briefing sessions for Street analysts invariably propel the stock price downward that day or the next morning. Even if the news and tone are positive, it has almost always been anticipated already in the prior days and weeks. The shares have run up with the expectation of favorable management comments. It is the same situation when executives do a road show and meet with several institutions one-on-one. The stock climbs weeks before such events and then begins to wane almost from the start of the meeting. There is rarely anything stunningly favorable announced at these sessions to drive the share price materially higher. Instead, usually there is a let down, nothing that specifically bullish, no occasion to raise earnings estimates or growth prospects, rarely enough to top the already upbeat expectation. Sometimes new negative elements or surprisingly cautious remarks surface, creating a downdraft in the shares.

Stop Loss Orders Can Protect Big Gains
But Are Mostly for Traders

Sharp appreciation, especially if within a brief 6–12 month interval, is valuable, a fortunate occurrence, so the temptation is to safeguard the profit. But investments also need to be long-term, leaving room for fluctuation. If you utilize a stop loss order after achieving a hefty gain, hopefully long-term, leave ample room on the downside, perhaps 30% below the current price. A stock that moves quickly from $15 to $50 can be protected with a stop loss at $35. Never give up a huge profit, as was so commonplace for all the naive amateur "investors" after the 1990s bubble burst. Gigantic losses are an outrage and must be prevented. But I use stop loss orders sparingly. Have your own mental stop loss levels to keep control. Have two selling price levels in mind for stocks that are underwater and where the outlook no longer warrants holding on. The first trigger price should be above the current level, though not all the way back to the purchase price, a palatable exit target that feels all right given that you are taking a loss on a poor investment. And the fail-safe protection mechanism to eliminate a disaster is a point that is below the existing price where you would feel bad but still avoid an enormous drubbing. Some of my best transactions have been of this nature—losers for sure—but I evaded a calamity.

Hedge Fund Positions Are a Source of Credible
Investment Ideas

You occasionally come across in the press or on TV interviews, the names of stocks held by a hedge fund. What gives them credence is that hedge fund managers have a direct personal stake. The partners are paid directly based on annual portfolio appreciation. Their bottom line is stock performance, no conflicting influences or bias like brokerage firms. In contrast, mutual fund managers are often rewarded based on asset size of their fund or capital inflow to their funds. And mutual fund performance is evaluated on a relative basis to market and sector indexes. Hedge funds only make money if their portfolios rise in value on an absolute basis. So their personal compensation is on the line. Their stock selections are impartial.

Yes, hedge funds often attempt to manipulate the stocks once a position is established—a hidden agenda to promote their long positions, a self-fulfilling prophecy—but they are true to their objectives.

Incidental Professional Stock Recommendations Are Problematic

If you run into a Street insider on an airplane or at a social function, any stock ideas you might obtain can be tricky. The same goes for company executives or other professionals who have some insight given their industry position. Their recommendation based on superior awareness or expertise may be a valid investment suggestion currently but can go stale in the future as situations change. Such an acquaintance is probably not there to advise you going forward; it's a one-shot opportunity. If their opinion reverses, or the scenario alters materially a year from now, you might never hear about it until it's too late. Even if you attempt to stay abreast of the story because you own the stock, you won't have the insight your contact had. Individuals can benefit initially from a stellar idea from a professional, but end up losing money later, if it collapses when the outlook reverses. The investor almost never has a timely heads up on the downside compared to the early tip at the beginning.

Technology Stocks Are a Huge Risk, a Maturing Industry

Most investors view high-tech stocks as exciting, high growth, wave of the future names where they might hit the jackpot. The image of Intel, Microsoft, Cisco, eBay, Amazon.com, and Google dance in their imaginations. Be supremely cautious. Tech is a maturing business. There is essentially no revenue growth at many of the established stalwarts. Smaller emerging companies are chased by institutions to excessive stock price levels. Product demand can shift quickly; quarterly order rate bookings can disappoint in a heartbeat. It's impossible to predict consistently. Competition is ferocious. Disruptive leapfrog developments undercut existing products and businesses. Markets get penetrated fast. There is ease of entry given all the venture capital money being tossed at the industry, amidst a dizzying amount of new venture investment pools formed over the last couple decades.

Technology stock prices move up on product cycle factors, positive earnings surprises, and during autumn—when hope for the new
year surfaces. But these are fleeting. The sector is overcovered by
Wall Street analysts, and their opinions keep shifting, adding to
volatility. The stocks are almost always overpriced. My friend, Ray
DeVoe, says it best, "Technology companies make lousy growth
stocks...you pay a high price for excitement and entertainment." If
you owned any of the major high-tech names in the Dow Jones Average from the market peak in 2000 through April 2007, you know what
I mean. They are 4 of the 10 worst performers among the 30 stocks,
declining as much as 68% (Intel) over that span. Vaunted Microsoft
slumped by 46%. High tech seems so enticing, scintillating, the avatar
of the last few decades as railroads were in the 1800s and automobiles
in the first half of the 20th century. But tech may be closer to the end
of its era than the beginning. These stocks should be viewed as short-
term trading vehicles.

Give Stock to Your Kids

The lessons to be learned by children in owning stocks are priceless.
Once my kids owned stocks and achieved some gains, they immediately became capitalists. It doesn't take kids long when looking up
their stock prices on the Internet to start asking questions about
which stocks to own, the reality of gains and losses, dividends, investing, business, and capital accumulation or savings. There is financial
training for life to be readily gleaned at an early stage when young-
sters actually feel the gravity of owning stocks. I let them help choose
the theme and even make mistakes in picking stocks. My son loved
model trains and real railroads, so I bought him a few shares of Union
Pacific. The education far outweighed any losses. I gave them my
alternatives or suggestions but allowed a wide berth for them to make
the call. It's even fun to have a competition: my stocks versus theirs.
I once talked to my daughter's 5th grade class about stocks by giving
them the annual reports of The Gap and The Limited. My kids are
long since out of college, but we still do this investing thing. My
daughter is a zingy, liberal, creative film writer and director, but she
still loves capital gains.

These guidelines are directives based on observations from over 32 years on the Street and more than 45 years of my own stock market investing. Tailor my investment principles and procedures to suit your personal profile: your age, work status, financial position, investment objectives, risk tolerance, and temperment. Your blue print may not be exactly the same as mine, depending on your own circumstances. But you need a direction, some order in your investing process. I find that most investors tend to flounder haphazardly, buffeted around by the Street like a boat adrift. What is missing is a good discipline. My recommended principles, strategies, and practices will provide this necessary investment regimen.

4

Evaluating Companies as Investment Candidates

Performing your own evaluation of companies that are investment candidates is a fairly straightforward activity. You do not have to be a rocket scientist. Be perspicacious. Get a feel for the character and profile of the corporation and its business. Always keep your antenna attuned. Opportunities to pick up intelligence and impressions on a company arise all the time. There are a number of ideal corporate attributes that serve as indicators of probable future achievement—uniqueness, focus, leadership, healthy finances, blue chip customers, conservative accounting, and consistency. The more of these I see, the more likely I am to have a favorable investment view. There is no such thing as the perfect company that demonstrates all the attributes I discuss here. But the more, the better. In judging future prospects, you must also assess the negatives, the flaws and defects, always subtle but more telling—companies get too broad, they overreach, neglect current clients, turnarounds never happen, over-centralization, dis-economies of scale. The dark side is important, as in many cases, it signals a no-go, and should discourage you from making a bad investment. Start with the positive end of the scale.

In the review process, always be attentive to any opportunity to gather intelligence on a company. I was jamming a pillow behind my back to get comfortable in a business class seat aboard a flight from Phoenix to Philadelphia. The noisy badinage among several pals-ey executives pertained to hospital and medical system topics. I spotted one of their carry-on bags with the letters SMS. It dawned on me that they probably worked at Shared Medical Systems, located in the suburbs outside Philly. That was a stock I covered. Following SMS was frustrating as there was little executive access and scant disclosures. The chatty, collegial SMS executive group on board tossed down libations and the decibels climbed. I realized that they were the top sales producers returning from the annual chairman's club revelry. I clammed up, grabbed a piece of scrap paper, and mentally amplified my virtual hearing aid volume.

Over the next couple hours, I heard about that company's problem contracts, new hospital client prospects, financial constraints, product and service issues, sales techniques to deceive management, derogatory views of top executives, and other highly intriguing revelations. To flush out a few of these topics, I cast myself as a computer systems consultant with barely even a passing academic interest. I was exceptionally familiar with the company, so I purposely couched my inquiries in general, bland terms to avoid raising any suspicions. And my note taking had to be undercover. Corporate executives in situations outside the office tend to have loose lips. Analysts never miss a chance to jabber with them in these conditions, to discover what's really happening. And my fortunate coincidence on the SMS flight added vastly to my understanding of the company.

Specialists Do It Better

The best companies have a specific forte and a narrow market concentration. In seeking investment candidates, look for companies that create their market, are there first, have a leading edge, and have an entrenched position. If the company is the second or third entrant in the market, it makes me cautious unless it is the leader of a specific narrow segment. The product or service must be differentiated. The company should be focused on a select, definable niche. Uniqueness may be in the customer base, selling approach, manufacturing, timing to market, or any other aspect. But there needs to be some kind of specialization story.

I love companies that are disciplined, that avoid veering off on market tangents. Diana Shipping is a Greek firm with ocean-going vessels transporting dry bulk commodities. When asked on its quarterly conference call why it did not do swaps of its ships and other financial transactions to enhance its results, management's reply was that they are a shipping company and are going to act like it. That's staying focused. When I started covering Concord EFS, it was only the fourth-largest credit card processor, but it was dominant in the emerging debit card sector, supermarkets, and gas stations, so it effectively gained share from the leader, First Data. The same could be said for Paychex.

No matter how flourishing the market, I shun also-rans. I prefer firms that are front-runners in their space, even if it's a narrow sector. Size is not an issue—I prefer small companies—but a company must be either the biggest player in its niche or demonstrably out in front of the competition. It should display leadership or a controlling market position. If it's a broad market, then it requires a far-reaching company to have the most sizeable share. Smaller companies can dominate minor or emerging sectors. While Automatic Data Processing dominates the payroll services market in broad, it's okay to be Paychex, which caters to the market of entities with less than 15 employees. It ranks third in size in payroll processing, is focused on the low end of the market, and has a distinct strength there. The tricky challenge for small specialist competitors is transforming and evolving as they outgrow their initial confined niches. They often attempt to break into adjunct markets already led by other participants rather than finding more original, virgin areas to pursue. Always be alert in determining when a company is outgrowing its sector. It may need to broaden and thus risk becoming less specialized.

Companies that are tightly focused, with a strict concentration, are more effective competitors than generalists. Those that become sizeable and broaden out into a wide-ranging market may have economic power and scale but lack flexibility, so it's more difficult to compete against narrowly aimed firms. It's like an 18-wheeler versus a sports car—the semi has heft, but it's not as fast and agile. Affiliated Computer Services could not go head to head against EDS or

Accenture in data center outsourcing and consulting. So it staked out the more specialized area of business process, paper-intensive, back-office outsourcing, a different area and an original, emerging market where it could be the primary player. IBM and others have now piled into this new area, but Affiliated, as a specialist, is in the forefront. Big generalists are boring and slow growth. Leave them to the mediocre mutual funds. You can do better.

Look for Stability and Consistency

A company with a steady stream of repetitive revenue can sustain its growth more predictably. It is easier to sustain a healthy growth pace when customers are an annuity stream, recurring revenue, rather than having to be replaced by new clients in the future. Computer services firms that I tracked had long-term contracts so they could rely on forthcoming guaranteed revenue in the current quarter and year ahead. Hardware and software companies have to book new business each quarter to generate revenue, allowing almost no visibility of the revenue stream even one quarter ahead. Oil pipeline companies generate revenue continuously from all their users, with no waiting to see what bookings might be signed during the current period. Sizeable new business prospects, repeat orders or contracts from existing customers, new market penetration, or accelerating demand for new products or services all lend a measure of predictability. I hate the uncertainty of having to hold my breath each quarter, hoping a company's orders were robust enough to achieve expected earnings. Stability and clarity are important to eliminate the roller coaster volatility in earnings and growth, a nightmare for investors.

Companies that generate reasonably consistent revenue and earnings growth performance connote good management, healthy markets, and a stalwart competitive position. I want to see dependable performance. It should not be a perfect clothesline, which would be highly suspect. You want to see truth in reporting, similar to Warren Buffet's style. In his words, "We won't smooth our quarterly or annual results: if earnings figures are lumpy when they reach headquarters, they will be lumpy when they reach you." It's not the absolute level of profits or the actual growth rate that's so important. Rather, it's the sustainability and dependability that counts.

The past record is important to evaluate a company's financial achievement during good and bad times. Although a certain degree of steadiness is a key measure, be suspect of perfection; it is usually faked and comes undone when least expected. An impeccable straight-line earnings record indicates inappropriate, myopic actions to overly massage and distort revenues and profits. It makes me nervous. Such even quarterly numbers do not reveal the real health of the business underneath the covers. Business patterns and trends are not perfectly smooth. The reality is that business is volatile. Companies have ample room to fudge, pad, or shave the numbers, and to a degree this is fine, but the results should reflect true business conditions. I trust growth records that fluctuate modestly, say gains of around 10% in difficult periods and expansion of over 20% in a favorable environment. Any wider variation than this means cyclicality—that is, a business that has big ups and downs depending on the economy. Business isn't always perfectly smooth flowing. It varies. Reported results reflect such deviation if they are credible. It requires manipulation to fashion perfectly smooth numbers.

Sales growth is the core engine, and without it, earnings gains are temporal, shallow, and probably financially managed. I like to see a solid double-digit revenue expansion pace, but nothing too excessive that would make it a challenge for management to maintain control and pose a difficult comparison the following year. Profit margins before taxes should also be double digits—high enough to reveal robust profitability but not so lofty as to be maxed out and unsustainable. Gradually rising margins are the ideal, adding operating leverage to obtain faster earnings improvement than the revenue expansion tempo. The tax rate should be full, over 30%. Any advance in profits that stems from reduced taxes is superficial. The income statement needs to be clean, void of special gains, recent write-down reserves being flowed back through, or other non-operational contributors.

Operating cash flow is similarly critical. The level should be highly positive. This is net income plus depreciation/amortization minus capital expenditures and dividends. Review the other less-important line items in the cash flow statement if material. Healthy companies should be generating cash. They cannot be outgrowing their internal financing capability. Income statement and cash flow accounting should be straightforward and conservative.

Earnings Quality and Conservative Accounting Are Paramount

Talk about a controversial topic these days. Accounting treatment is the culprit behind countless debacles during the last few years. If financial statements have too many footnotes, your antenna should rise. Pro forma earnings, so prevalent, bear extreme scrutiny. Income statements with too many "exceptional" items that need to be pro forma-ed out are suspect. Inspect footnotes for commitments and contingencies. Earnings should be pure with no so-called one-time factors. Look at operating earnings to understand what's really occurring. Is the company disclosing a far higher level of profits in its shareholder statements than it is reporting to the IRS for taxes? Revenue recognition is subject to particularly flagrant manipulation. Contracts can be booked in varying manners, and despite now more restrictive guidelines, there is still room for a measure of upfront revenue recognition and under-recording current costs. Percentage-of-completion accounting is hairy and wide open to abuse.

Big upfront reserves, established when making an acquisition, are another bothersome practice that results in a slush fund to manage future earnings. Off-balance sheet financing is a handy way to hide true indebtedness or liability levels. Read the footnotes here; add the debt back in. Examine the fine print for accounting mischief—inventory valuation, pension fund accounting, deferred taxes, and reserves for doubtful accounts. The issuance of options, in reality a future liability, also gives me pause. Use of options should be modest. They are dilutive to the future earnings stream, and investors should care. I don't want to see any of this stuff, and if evident, a deeper probe is mandatory.

Misleading pro forma, adjusted smoothing of earnings results, is the key manner in which corporate executives alter reality. Adjusted, normalized, reconfigured, or perfunctory earnings give me a pause. Pro forma is great fiction in a perfect world. It's the way management delivers expected results for investors despite innumerable cross currents and setbacks. Any train-wrecked company can show beautiful numbers this way. The quantitative level of a "one-time" factor can be detailed, but let analysts and investors conjure up their own adjusted earnings results. We don't need executives propounding this fiction. One-time hits and write-offs have become so commonplace, they need to be factored into PE multiples and stock price valuations. Despite the current requirement to report GAAP earnings, most companies are also emphasizing the window-dressed, suspect "pro forma" number to virtually eliminate the constant array of negative (sometimes even positive) impacts. And I am bothered by earnings restatements, too. This is like rewriting history, and carries accounting implications. In 2005, there were around 1,200 such restatements. Revenues are no exception. Some companies try to smooth this out to portray steadier progress by deferring revenue, recording unbilled revenue, using flaky receivable terms—all sorts of techniques. Revenue recognition must be tightened and simplified, maybe even to the extent of reporting only revenue actually collected in cash that quarter.

The Google IPO offering statement indicated its intention to reflect current reality in its interim earnings reports, which is a refreshingly honest approach. Google's IPO Owner's Manual for potential IPO investors claimed "outside pressures too often tempt companies to sacrifice long-term opportunities to meet quarterly expectations. Sometimes this pressure has caused companies to manipulate financial results in order to 'make their quarter.' " It went on to say, "we are not able to predict our business within a narrow range for each quarter. A management team distracted by a series of short-term targets is as pointless as a dieter stepping on a scale every half hour."

Google does not give earnings forecast guidance. The company's strategy is to continue concentrating on the long-term even if that has short-term financial impacts. Google's founders stated in the prospectus that "they would remain risk takers, willing to place bets that had only a 10% chance of earning a billion dollars over a long period of time." The bottom line is that Google is trying to avoid the insane, artificial, quarterly treadmill of ironing out all the legitimate, normal kinks in results that most companies foist on investors to pretend perfection.

Executives play down the negatives and accentuate the more upbeat factors by many other subtle techniques. Explanation of key financial items is usually buried in latent filings. Such detail is normally disclosed in lengthy, boring, belated SEC 10-Q and 10-K reports that are published sometimes a month or two after the reporting date. It is lost and forgotten by that time. Simple, balanced, truthful elucidation of important financial items on the balance sheet and cash flow statements are rarely placed in earnings releases, a detriment to full disclosure and investor understanding. This clarification should be especially required of numbers that have altered materially since the last reporting period. I covered a company whose financials became increasingly skewed, moving in ominous directions. The extent and the true cause, a massive contract that was out of control, running awry, was not fully revealed or detailed for a couple years. It was material. It should have been disclosed on a timely basis. Pertinent portions of the comprehensive 10-Q and 10-K text should be condensed and contained in quarterly earnings releases.

Healthy, Solid Balance Sheet Is a Must

Finances should be like Fort Knox, with maximum flexibility to finance future activities. There should be nothing flaky or out of whack. I start with cash; a hefty level is key. Then debt—preferably none, but at most, debt should not total more than 20% of capitalization. This is the debt-to-capitalization ratio, debt as measured against the total of debt and stockholders' equity. Maybe 50% is acceptable depending on the type of business. The need to service too much debt with burdensome interest payments is a pressure on earnings. Accounts receivable should be under tight control, 60–90 days sales outstanding, and no adverse, rising trend. Inventory levels are to be under similar control. Next are unusual items that serve as a warning, like unbilled revenue, deferred costs, bulky accounts payable, and different classes of common stock. If any of these factors exist, they must be thoroughly assessed and clearly understood.

Pay Attention to the Dark Side

The dark side of a corporation is usually more obscure, more subtle. Attributes are easier to identify because corporate executives and their steroid-driven marketing and PR departments work overtime to publicize the positives. And favorably biased Wall Street research also constantly emphasizes the upbeat aspects. Having reviewed hundreds of companies, I have observed certain corporate defects that seem to crop up repeatedly, decade after decade, as companies come and go. When these faults pop up in my appraisal process, they make me guarded. Serious blemishes are often the seeds of destruction. They are usually not obvious, and management always cloaks them in a favorable light, rendering them more benign on the surface. Investors should be wary of companies displaying such imperfections.

Generalists Do It Worse

This is the corollary to "specialists do it better." One of the more readily identifiable characteristics that I find off-putting is a company that is a generalist. In this era of specialization, narrow focus, and niches, companies lose this advantage as they expand and broaden. Size often leads to being a generalist, which renders a company susceptible to emerging niche players grabbing market share and exploiting new areas. Generalist giants fight a defensive battle, protecting their established market and client base. They are fearful of destroying the existing product or service, rendering it obsolete, so they become stodgy, setting themselves up to be toppled as markets and technologies change. They become boring. They lose their cutting edge, and their creative, risk-taking personnel. They can hang on for a long time, giving the appearance of dominant leadership stability, but are vulnerable to a thousand cuts by single-concentration competitors that eventually push the generalist into oblivion. Specialists lead new market waves. Almost all new markets and developments are pioneered by up-and-comer firms aimed in a single direction. Eventually, these winners get oversized, become generalists, and lose out in the next major market inflection point. If a long explanation is necessary to describe a firm's business, it's a generalist. Assume that its prospects are lackluster.

My experience in covering the technology industry for over three decades is that once firms become huge, they stagnate, become ponderous, get too broad, make decisions by committee, are inhibited by consensus, lose touch, and constantly plan or strategize rather than execute and act. They just plain run out of steam. It's difficult to attract invigorated, creative, excited employees to a massive bureaucracy. Good workers depart, and laggards hang around. The complexity is too much to manage. Such supertankers take too long to turn in new directions, are usually late in shifting with markets, and are easy targets.

Bigness to me connotes dinosaurs, with a few exceptions like General Electric and Wal-Mart. But even GE can only grow at the rate of the economy. General Motors stood still as Toyota blew by it like Hurricane Katrina. Toyota is big but focused. By keeping a narrow concentration, Whole Foods is making established supermarket chains look like lumbering giants. Size is a constraint to growth and carries with it dis-economies of scale. Most big companies are cumbersome; they are just waiting to become extinct. We analysts are always told of the advantages of size, market share, market power, and dominance. In reality, it's quite the opposite. Smaller firms have better cost controls, are more flexible, and tend to be more niched. They lead the new developments and market changes. And smaller companies with more dynamic growth attract the best personnel. Investors should not be led astray by companies that claim their mammoth size is a favorable attribute. Great corporate bulk is usually a negative.

Centralized Control Can Get Out of Control Overnight

A common flaw to be wary of is dominant, heavy-handed, overly controlling top management. It fosters wimpy yes-man executives outside the corner office. Although it's fine for particularly small companies to have a heavily centralized management structure, most firms sizeable enough to be publicly held stocks should be fairly decentralized. Companies and markets quickly outgrow a concentrated top management's ability to make all the choices. An ivory tower group loses touch with lower levels. The problem is shifting from an initial core top management decision-making setup to later on entrusting others to run operations, call shots, and steer in opportunistic new directions. This transition is especially acute when the founder is still present. Founders rarely yield control until it's too late.

Centralized control is smooth and effective, lulling investors to sleep thinking it's good management, until overnight material problems hit like a flash flood. The executives at the top, thinking only they were qualified to micromanage most aspects of the company, find they were unaware of massive underlying issues or threats that finally become manifest. Centralized control appears to work fine to outsiders until it doesn't anymore. It's like a dictatorship—more polished and practical than a messy democracy. But things can collapse quickly when the top is strong while the supporting structure is weak.

A Dramatic Acquisition During Troubled Times Is a Diversionary Tactic

Sometimes executives, realizing that the company is in trouble, lethargic, losing market share, mature, growth diminished, and earnings outlook murky, embark on a desperate path. They attempt an inappropriate leapfrog—a dramatic, major acquisition to mask the condition. This is a sure warning. Companies running out of gas, realizing it will be impossible to maintain the expected expansion and profitability that underpins the current stock price, have a tendency to go a bridge too far. The purpose of a monster acquisition under these circumstances is to muddy the water, tossing financials and operating income statements into complexity, and obscuring current operating numbers. It sets up a situation where executives conjure up a *strategic* story for the future. There is the promise of enhanced results stemming from the stunning deal. Profit improvement via *synergism* and duplicate cost elimination are always a year or more away, but investors are told to be patient. By making a titanic, splashy merger, executives can forestall the need for immediate earnings, covering up an imminent earnings shortfall. Such a measure is overreaching. It's a disguise.

The Daimler takeover of Chrysler in 1998 is a good illustration of the danger signal sounded when executives attempt a gigantic pole vault act to offset doldrums in the rest of the business. It was struggling, so it laid out $36 billion for a deteriorating U.S. also-ran. Nine years later, Daimler coughed up another half billion to get a private-equity firm to take it away...a mere $37 billion mistake. Carly Fiorina's frantic move at Hewlett-Packard also fit this mold. To stir up the pot amidst her stumbling turnaround efforts, she acquired Compaq, a flagging PC producer. Compaq's poor financials and eroding market share cast it as a fading player looking to be bailed out. Carly caught flack from several quarters, including the Hewlett Foundation, for attempting this distress tactic, barely obtaining enough shareholder votes. It made little sense, doubling up in a lousy business, but her viraginous style held sway, at least until she was proven wrong a couple years later. Warren Buffet's view of companies that move into stressed markets was pointed out in Fortune Magazine's article on the failure of the Compaq deal three years later: "When a management with a reputation for brilliance tackles a business with a reputation for bad economics, it is usually the reputation of the business that remains intact."

AT&T committed a similar blunder when it was in the doldrums in the 1980s. A splashy acquisition was proposed as just the antidote to lead it to recovery. Sure. The spurious idea was to vault into the computer industry as an adjunct to telecom services. A regulated long distance carrier in the competitive high-tech industry? I realized the extent of the farce at a conference when I heard an AT&T in-house techy describe the search process. The extensive evaluation listed 11 computer company possibilities from best to worst fit. NCR was last on the list. But the chairman decided otherwise, and launched an unfriendly takeover for NCR. AT&T ended up way overpaying, the graft-on was a failure, AT&T's chairman was replaced, and NCR was later written down and spun off at a huge loss. A debacle. Predictable. Just another attempt to dig out of trouble by a diversionary tactic.

Sometimes the deflection tactic may not be an acquisition. It could be a dazzling move into a radically new market, as when a consumer PC software firm launches into the corporate market. Or the leap might be a striking shift in the business model, such as a computer services company deciding to sell software. Spectacular actions are often convenient cover-ups for near-term financial underperformance. Executives refer to the transition costs as temporary. Analysts and investors are directed to cool their heels and await the big payoff, which rarely happens. Those naive enough to hang on for the glorious outcome end up being disappointed. Such measures are overreaching. They are an act of desperation and lead, at the minimum, to a mess for a few years.

Managements and boards love acquisitions in the pursuit of the Holy Grail—gigantic size. It makes them feel more important; they obtain more clout and more pay. Most of the time, the justification is fallacious, things like synergy or economies of scale. Look at America Online's deal for Time Warner and Quest's takeover of U.S. West. Management made them sound like good ideas at the time. The bigger the better was the byword. But sizeable companies making an acquisition to get even bigger is a death knell. Instead, they should be divesting and downsizing to become more streamlined.

Customer Base Should Be Hardy and Vigorous

I prefer companies that address thriving, vigorous companies as clients, customers that are expanding, and have good profitability and money to spend. This provides a good tailwind as compared to the uphill battle when involved with depressed end markets. Lucrative industries like banking, energy, or pharmaceuticals are preferable sectors to serve, compared with stodgy areas like education and government. Commercial markets yield higher profit margins and faster growth than government or heavily regulated industries. If it's a consumer business, the end market should be abundant and flush. I always ascertain the quality of a company's client base. Are there major contracts with customers teetering on the verge of bankruptcy? Is there heavy dependency on a few sizeable clients that are floundering? Or is the customer base comprised of firms like GE, Coca-Cola, Merck, or Citicorp?

An element that executives usually overemphasize is new business. Pursuing and landing new contracts is exciting for corporate leaders, but sometimes this is accompanied by neglect of existing clients. Executing on existing contracts and satisfying current clients is boring. This operational drudgery is the heart and soul of building a flourishing business, referrals, add-ons, rising profits as contracts mature, and follow-on revenue. But it's not sexy and gets little internal corporate kudos. The high-profile acclaim goes to salespersons and teams bringing in new deals, especially mega-sized contracts or big Fortune 100 names as customers. Stocks trade higher on sizzling press releases proclaiming impressive new clients and contracts. Management is consumed by this siren song, declaring the new business as a building block for future growth. The problem is that once obtained, the clients may be taken for granted, underserved, and shuffled to managers that were not part of the initial selling effort when empty promises were made.

Analysts normally do customer checks when initiating coverage of a company, but tend not to follow up to ascertain customer satisfaction later on. It's critical. This cancer can spread quietly and be overlooked for a long time, but client neglect will eventually surface and bring a company to its knees, like General Motors and Ford. I remember one time in the mid-1980s, IBM stressed its major theme as "the year of the customer." At its massive four-day user conference that year, the chairman failed to make an appearance to schmooze with customers or even make a speech. It told me everything. The subsequent new chairman brought in from the outside altered this type of behavior. New deals are cool and can be catalysts. Investors can get wowed by new sales, but it's more difficult to determine the quality of existing client caretaking. Tending to current clients is real work. Companies that execute these operational aspects may appear dull but are solid and enduring.

Established, Entrenched Companies Stand Pat

Managements want to book new business all right, but rarely are they willing to take the risk of leapfrogging their current market offering. A common corporate mindset is to protect the base, and avoid impacting existing business or obsolescing current client installations. Companies become defensive once successful, and are afraid of change. This is often the case when founders stick around or where firms have reached spectacular heights in their initial focused business thrust. As an analyst, I always want to see companies making changes and doing creative new things, never standing still even though the current business is robust.

The natural tendency is to stand pat, make minor adjustments and improvements, and protect the base. Xerox, with its copiers in the 1970s, was a classic example. Digital Equipment in minicomputers was another case. EDS suffered by sticking with its core expertise, datacenter outsourcing, as that sector matured. Meanwhile, upstart competitors led the charge into business back-office process outsourcing. The supermarket chains missed the shift to healthier food. Detroit automakers overlooked the trend toward hybrid cars. Just as analysts often miss market inflection points, so do companies. It's difficult for entrenched enterprises to admit that there is a market or technological shift beginning to occur that imperils their existing business. They go into a defensive posture and, like an NFL football team protecting a lead late, play prevent defense, giving up 10 yards per play hoping the clock expires. It usually means prevent victory.

Turnarounds Just Don't Work Over Time

Once a company has lost its edge, deteriorated, and earnings shortfalls ensue, the normal response by the board is to replace management. The new team champions a turnaround. Financial restructurings, yes. Downsizings, divestitures, and mergers, maybe. New managements typically storm into troubled companies, hire fresh executive teams, promise massive change, make a myriad of moves, take jarring write-offs and reserves, and slash costs, often with improved investor communications. All the excitement and attempted transformation get heavy press and analyst attention. Compared with the deep pit of the past, these seemingly innovative actions are alluring to investors. But they never pan out to the point where the company really transitions into a flourishing leadership role again.

I was skeptical of Carly Fiorina's efforts to overhaul Hewlett-Packard, especially after she jammed the mega-acquisition of Compaq. What did I say earlier about desperate leapfrogs? Guess the board didn't think her efforts were panning out either. The old, original AT&T, as its business degenerated, employed many new CEOs to embark on turnarounds, and finally succumbed by itself being aquired. Xerox has struggled with a half dozen efforts to transition and re-energize itself over the last 25 years.

Richard Brown failed miserably to turn EDS, and met his defenestration. The company's follow-on management 2 years later was still trying to regain some growth. With little to show by early 2005 and another year of struggle ahead, what carrot could it dangle at its analyst meeting? That's easy. Promise some boxcar bookings way down the road. It flashed $23 billion in anticipated orders for 2007, hoping analysts would forget the dismal 2004 new contract total of under $15 billion, the maturing industry, overseas competition, and all the other adverse influences. That was far enough out to avoid scrutiny for a long time. It's tough enough to predict next quarter, let alone 3 years in the future. Outlandish, distant promises amidst ongoing setbacks are a clear signal that the foreseeable turnaround outlook is floundering.

Turnaround promises always entail investors waiting a couple years or longer. There are various hopeful milestones. Sometimes managements shore up the situation, declare victory, and merge the company. That's the best case. Milking a company for cash flow and improving the financial structure are also doable. But sinking ships do not resurface as forward attack position aircraft carriers. Don't expect a dramatic metamorphosis or reinvigorated growth. Turnarounds never manifest such results.

Opulence and Luxuriousness Are an Alarm Bell

As an investor always be on guard for companies that display off-putting traits. One of the most obvious is sumptuous digs, or living high on the hog. I am turned off by companies that have exceptionally luxurious offices. I make note of the deep pile carpeting, glass, artwork and plush furniture when I visit headquarters. The same for art and furniture. If it's too extravagant, it indicates an attitude that executives are in it mostly for themselves. It's almost a sure thing that when companies create a vast new headquarters campus, they are set up for a fall. The rationale is always employee proximity, even economics. In reality, it's usually an upgrade on the lavishness scale. This is sometimes conspicuous in the annual report.

My first lesson in shying away from companies that build lavish new home office facilities was Xerox in the 1970s. The chairman and early founder Peter McCullough proudly paraded a big analyst group, which had arrived an hour before the meeting started, on a full tour of the new building in Stamford, Connecticut. Highlighted prominently were the rich parquet floors, the employees' gym, and assorted marble, brass, mahogany, and other plush features. We walked around stupefied, realizing that management had built a posh monumental palace in which to bask. Although the new headquarters may not have been a direct cause, this display of superficial financial prosperity turned out to be a good warning sign of the checkered record that ensued over subsequent decades.

Other signs of splendor are the executive automobile fleet, number and use of corporate aircraft, corporate country club memberships, stadium corporate suites, the corporate name on stadiums, flying first class, staying at Four Seasons hotels, designer suits, exclusive executive dining rooms, excessive pricey client and employee entertainment or outings, and even the location of analyst meetings. It bothers me when the annual analyst briefing session is held at a posh resort or country club location, encompassing golf and spa activities.

John Chambers, the CEO of Cisco Systems, is a fabulous representation of the opposite extreme, an egalitarian with a humble management style that all investors should hold dear. He has no corner office, he has a 12-by-12-foot space in the center of the floor with no view. The outside window offices are for lower-level employees; management is located in the middle. This atmosphere indicates to employees that they are important, and it stimulates communications. Conference tables are round to convey equality rather than a hierarchical structure. A nice message to underpin worker moral. His desk has a laminate top, chairs have plastic arms, his modest West Virginia background comes through. There are no reserved parking spaces and no special executive office pecking order.

Be Cautious of Excessive Hype and Promotion

This portrays superficiality, an emphasis on façade over substance. Some companies have massive marketing machines, churning out press releases daily on the most inconsequential, immaterial matters. The investor relations contact might as well be from a publicity firm, has meager, specific information on the company's operations or outlook, and blithely espouses favorable generic commentary to investors. We analysts come away after a meeting or conversation like we've just had a meal of Chinese food, still feeling empty. A marketing, press, and advertising blitz is a distracting cover-up, a smokescreen. Glossy, overly fancy, expensive annual reports are off-putting, too much show. I look for understated content, meaningful discussion, not glamour. Real companies with depth do not need excessive boosterism. A plethora of announcements make analysts and investors tune out, so when there is an important message, it is diminished. When I see executives making too many public showings, press interviews, and media appearances, I wonder who's minding the store. It also makes me question their intentions. Are they managing the company or the stock? Is management attempting to manipulate a favorable perception in fear of outsiders realizing the truth? Companies with hyperactive publicity campaigns lack substance.

A former director of investor relations at Tyco International during the days of Dennis Kozlowski's errant personal spending binge testified in court to this promotional conduct. According to court testimony, his investor relations unit indicated it was pushed into becoming "the marketing department for the company's stock." Knowing that "the function of investor relations is to provide true and accurate information," Tyco's approach with analysts and investors was instead "to highlight and accentuate the positives and mitigate the negatives."

Executives can be vague and ambivalent, always putting a favorable cast on the outlook. At one analyst meeting, the chairman of a beleaguered company was quoted as saying, "Growth is both our challenge and our biggest goal." He went on to compound the confusion when blurting "by cutting overhead, we can grow our business." This style strains credibility and generates distrust. Cost reduction aids profitability but it requires new orders and sales to attain revenue expansion.

Companies can further distort the picture by slanting and spinning earnings results presentations. Typical press releases pertaining to a stunning earnings drop carry a headline rubric like "Revenues climb x%, New Contract Prospects Encouraging"—no reference in the caption to the massively disappointing plunge in profits or the reason behind the tanking. This is a misleading disclosure. If the news is negative, it should be portrayed that way and fully detailed. Executives commonly pull the wool over the eyes of the investing public with cagey, manipulative releases. Press announcements seldom detail the uncertainties and risks involved in any favorable announcement such as a new contract. Equal time is never given to the challenges and issues during formal conference calls and briefing sessions. An almost-universal practice is to willingly discuss positive news in detail, but avoid drilling down to the minutiae on disappointing setbacks. The same goes for late-day conference calls to spell out bad news, the hope being that Wall Street will have already gone home and that press coverage will be limited due to nearing deadlines. It's curious how only the buoyant news is described ad nauseam on calls conducted conveniently during primetime to encourage the widest possible audience.

Be Wary of Stock Buybacks and Dilutive Stock Options

Stock repurchase plans, when a company buys back its shares in the open market, are a patently pathetic action to artificially boost earnings and the stock price. Executives rarely announce such deals when business is ripping, the outlook is brilliant, and the stock is running. Buybacks usually occur when profits have stalled or the stock price has languished. This type of financial maneuvering is no substitute for growth, market share, and the more real catalysts to propel a stock. These days companies are even borrowing, issuing debt, and leveraging the balance sheet to repurchase stock. It is shortsighted, and it makes me suspect. Home Depot, its business affected by the nose dive in the housing market, is a case in point. It issued debt and launched a whopping repurchase of 25% of its shares in June 2007. Wal-Mart, its stock price having flat-lined for about a year, commenced a $15 billion buyback at the same time. Be cautious when companies are borrowing, selling assets, and buying back their shares. It only works for a little while.

Dilutive stocks options issuing rights to employees to purchase shares far in the future at the price fixed on the grant date, are another unfavorable element. There is a quantifiable dilution to potential earnings per share when millions of stock options are issued. Shareholders need to be more aware of this impact, and executives have to be constrained from what has become flagrantly excessive compensation. Mandating that the full effect on earnings be calculated and reported is advancing the goal of reporting legitimate, genuine results. It puts a damper on this lucrative freebie that, until recently, has been all one way—at the shareholders expense. When a stock price plummets and options are vastly underwater, corporate executives and employees deftly dodge this personal loss by the reissuance of new options at the lower price. Too bad stockholders can't re-do their purchase price after the drop. Need I even mention the proliferation of past unsavory, basically illegal backdating of stock options? Another ploy to enrich executives at the expense of investors. Too many executives want it both ways.

Stock option policies are overly liberal because of the past "freebie" accounting treatment. Broadcom is just one of endless examples of heavy option issuance. Though incurring almost $1 billion in red ink in 2003 and negative retained earnings of almost $7 billion at the end of that year, it proposed an option plan in early 2004 equivalent to 12% of its enterprise value, diluting current shareholders by almost 4%. And it had previously reissued lower-priced options after the initial ones dropped way underwater in 2001 and again in 2003.

Brocade Communications was another poster child illustrating excessive distribution of options. Its stock came public in 1999 at $4.75 per share; by October 2000 it reached $133, and it now trades in single figures again. The former CEO of Brocade was indicted by federal prosecutors for defrauding shareholders relating to the company's stock options timing practices and was convicted in a criminal trial in mid-2007. Egregiously using options as the drug of choice over the years like many tech companies, it announced in early 2005 that it was restating its results for the prior 6 years, every year it was public, due to errors in its option accounting. It recorded added compensation charges relating to option grants, and its 2004 net loss was $32 million instead of the $2 million it originally announced. Hewlett-Packard's shareholders voted in 2004 in favor of expensing all options, but management didn't listen and continued to overlook the initial potential dilutive impact in financial reports until accounting regulations changed, requiring such treatment.

I am on the side of Berkshire Hathaway in this option debate. It has never issued stock options. Warren Buffet, its leader, is a high-profile proponent of expensing options. He also believes that when options are exercised, there should be restrictions on executives from selling the shares for a reasonably long period of time. Microsoft recently decided to no longer grant options. The Financial Accounting Standards Board started requiring options granted by corporations to be fully expensed on the earnings statement beginning in the spring of 2006. Now we're seeing such grants shrink quickly...gee, what a surprise. Yes, stock prices may, to a degree, already discount potential future stock option dilution if a company is particularly generous or stingy in its option issuance. But it harkens back to a similar situation when a company completed a huge purchase acquisition, adding enormous revenues and earnings along with massive amortization expense. I heard the argument so often that we analysts and investors should overlook the amortization cost that impacts reported earnings and concentrate on operating earnings, including all the earnings contributed by the acquired entity. Corporate executives wanted it both ways. I hear the same case from management desiring to treat options like they are free.

As an investor, you should always be a skeptic, searching for a company's vulnerability. It's easy to spot the brilliance, the excellence of a corporation. Wall Street, company executives, and even the press spout these superlatives constantly. The flaws are hidden, and there are a plethora of interests who have a major stake in keeping them covered up. So the challenge is to identify the concealed shortcomings that may be a deal breaker for an investor.

5

Executive Traits Are a Revealing Investment Gauge

A critical part of the investment appraisal and company evaluation process is gauging management effectiveness, quality, character, and values. Surprisingly, this essential aspect is often disregarded by the Street, unconcerned with character differences among the companies it covers. In crucial moments when events panic investors and stocks nose dive, executives are usually temporarily incommunicado. The ultimate basis of a judgment call in those circumstances is whether management can be trusted. It also holds true over the long-term. Who would you rather invest in, trustworthy or cagey executives? You need to get a handle on executive values in companies where you have an investment.

On occasion I had the opportunity to size up executives during a round of golf. I gained more insight observing and schmoozing with executives over 18 holes than I could ever obtain in a meeting. A struggling high-end payroll processor pre-announced a disappointing earnings shortfall the day before my annual investor conference started in Miami. The stock tanked, and the executives were blistered by investors at their sessions. Then it happened again the next year. Because he was from the Midwest and it was January, the CEO stuck

around after the conference for golf with me on the Blue Monster at
the Doral, where my confab was centered. I assigned the portfolio
manager from the biggest mutual fund holder of the stock to our
foursome. He brutalized the unfortunate executive for 2½ hours with
caustic jabs. After 9 holes, I started to switch the CEO's clubs from
my cart onto that investor's buggy. The CEO stopped me cold,
beseeching "Don't do this to me, my round's already ruined!" That
showed me humility and good natured genuineness, a good guy I
could trust.

Wall Street analysts deal with such an array of corporate executives over the years that when we confront the next one, there is usually
a fit with some past style or type. We observe executives and can
almost predict a company's future from previous experiences with
similar management at other firms. Investors, too, can sometimes
spot such traits and behavior in their pursuit of potential investment
opportunities and in staying abreast of their current holdings.

There are a number of recurring styles and molds—some are
constructive and others are detrimental. Many times executives are
not lying; they are just uninformed, naive, or overly optimistic. They
can be eternal lowballers, always in a hype mode, taciturn, or shrewd
storytellers. Investors need to identify good executive traits and undesirable ones. Executives make common mistakes when problems surface, repeated so often by different companies over the decades. You
need to be aware of these blunders as they occur; they probably mean
the future will only get worse for a while.

Listen to Executives on Conference Calls

Individual investors do not have the access to executives that is available to many Street insiders. Just about the only way to get firsthand
exposure to management is by listening in on quarterly conference
calls. You can hear the executives' prepared remarks and their
answers to questions live by webcast or telephone. These calls are
scheduled a week or two in advance of earnings results and are publicly
announced in a company press release. If you need more details, such
as telephone access numbers, call investor relations at the company.
A replay is normally available for another a week or so after the call.

The sessions are available to everyone on a listen-only mode, but only Street analysts and institutional investors can ask the executives direct questions.

A conference call is worth a thousand reports. This is where you will obtain some feel for the company's management style and character. It's like observing a press conference. Judge the level of confidence and conviction, arrogance or humbleness, candor, conservativeness, and other characteristics. Take note of the executives' temper. Sometimes they sound hesitant or unconvincing. You will get some help in drawing out the management from the questions presented by analysts who often act like piranhas. Important and revealing elements can be uncovered. Beyond just observing management traits, these calls are exceedingly valuable to gain insight on a company's business, current trends, and outlook. They are more useful than research reports to discover countervailing analyst attitudes, and key Street concerns and uncertainties. Read between the lines to determine the real message. And pay attention to other more subtle aspects of these calls. You can glean as much from the nuances as from the actual remarks. Take note of the executive commentary for tone, length, and other elements. Prepared remarks can drone on for 45 minutes, leaving only a brief 15-minute segment for Q & A. That may indicate a cover-up to dodge penetrating questions and cross examination. Get an overall impression. Is the picture clear and favorable, or clouded and uncertain? These calls provide the closest look you'll ever get at a company.

The Visionary Leader or Founder Who Adapts

This management type is rare and relatively easy to spot. These individuals define each corporate era and will be remembered 50 years from now. Analysts feel honored that they have the privilege of knowing such leaders and experiencing first hand the emergence of these exceptional companies. Bill Gates of Microsoft, Robert Noyce at Intel, Ross Perot from EDS, and possibly Larry Ellison with Oracle, are illustrative of this category, where I had personal contact and research coverage. You can add to the list Warren Buffet, Jack Welch, Steve Jobs, John Chambers (Cisco), and companies like FedEx and

Wal-Mart. Bill Hewlett was another example. I'll never forget the twice-a-year New York analyst meetings held by Hewlett-Packard in the 1970s. Hewlett, who created HP in a garage with David Packard, would preside for over 4 hours on stage, straight-talking from the heart. He didn't shy away from the negative concerns. It was a thorough working session, no-nonsense. He had credibility.

What distinguishes these founders or leaders is that they transform, adapt, and broaden as their fledgling start-ups become dominant worldwide juggernauts, or they take their giant firms in reinvigorating new directions. Bill Gates has taken Microsoft from PC operating systems, to PC applications, to business software, on into the Internet, and now into games and entertainment. He just keeps transforming and broadening with the markets. Visionaries identify a new market, create it, lead it, and shift their company's direction as the sector matures. And they are charismatic leaders, colorful, outspoken, driven, creative, aggressive, fearless, and exceedingly self-confident.

Listening to such executives is enthralling. When I questioned Bill Gates during coffee breaks at meetings, he would rock back and forth, swaying on his feet, mulling questions in his mind several seconds, and then articulating brilliant, balanced answers. The more unassuming and genuine the executive, like Gates and Noyce, the more convincing are their comments. But you must also avoid hero worship, being ensorcelled, blindly believing these executives' spiels without critical assessment. This is a challenge for analysts and investors who can fall into a true believer trap. When this type is arrogant, with an attitude, analysts have a more natural and healthy skepticism. But the common thread is that all these leaders build enormously winning companies over a long period of time.

Sometimes Founders are Boom-Bust

This genre of leader is an inspired, inventive creator of a dynamic, dazzling company that is a big winner for a while, but they can overstay their time. As markets shift, times change, and the company matures, this pioneer is stuck in the original business that eventually hits the wall. The early vision that drove the firm to great heights crests, but this mastermind is blind, defending the established business instead of going in new directions. He overstays his time. Business history is littered with examples. Some I have dealt with as an analyst were Peter McCullough at Xerox, Scott McNealy of Sun Microsystems, Ken Olsen of Digital Equipment, Charles Wang at Computer Associates, William Norris of Control Data, and Jim Sprague with National Semiconductor.

The challenge for investors is to recognize founder executives who, while they are still in the boom period, may eventually end up in this category. Watch emerging companies with innovative approaches that represent a potential threat to established market leaders. Founders are vulnerable once their firms become pre-eminent. They pooh-pooh competitive warnings, are overly defensive and entrenched in the existing strategy, and are unwilling to cannibalize the current business in order to stay on the leading edge. Founders seldom change, but markets and technologies move on. Ken Olsen at Digital, in reaction to the emergence of the personal computer in the early 1980s stridently pronounced that his firm would not participate in that business—"the PC was only a toy!" He developed "serious" computers. It's ironic that after his company crumbled, it was absorbed by Compaq. The future becomes history, and these companies remain fixated on their early dominant lead. Like ostriches, they don't see or want to acknowledge that their original, wonderful product or service is becoming mature or obsolete. After founders preside over their own bust, they are replaced by turnaround executives, usually to no avail.

Founders Can't Perform Magic Twice

Be wary of founders who have created one winner, and then move on to launch another start-up in a different area. The assumption is that they can build a second big winner given their reputation of achievement the first time. Their initial breakthrough was a confluence of the right market circumstances, product/service, timing, and other factors. It is not possible to bring together all these catalysts perfectly for an encore. Serendipity cannot be planned or recreated. Analysts and investors are often fooled by a founder's gleaming reputation and thus seduced into believing lightening can strike twice. This was impressed on me back in the 1980s when Gene Amdahl, instrumental in creating generations of mainframe computers at IBM, had launched a stellar start-up company, Amdahl, to develop IBM knock-off computers for a drastically cheaper price. With his Amdahl achievement, he embarked on an attempt to repeat the triumph, a new company called Trilogy Systems. No computer technology ever surfaced from its laboratory, and it quickly faded into oblivion. There can sometimes be modest achievement with the next go around, but never expect to match the pinnacle of the first time. Be cautious when these founders' egos lead them to try repeating the magic.

The Classic Operator, Realist, and No-Nonsense Driver

This is another favorable executive style. These are typically chief operating officers. Sometimes they are chairman who succeed founders but still manage their company as operators rather than as magnetic, imaginative leaders. They are tough, organized, detailed, quick studies, decision makers, serious, hard-working, and unafraid to confront any senior executive. Steve Ballmer of Microsoft, and in the past Lou Gerstner of IBM, Ray Lane of Oracle, and Josh Westin of Automatic Data Processing are cases in point that I am familiar with. When Josh was head of ADP, he ran a tight ship. I remember when I was meeting with other executives at the headquarters, he requested to see me for five minutes. As I marched into his office, he stated his question would take one minute, that I'd have two minutes to respond, leaving two minutes for me to have one counter question and a reply. As I exited, a glimpse at my watch indicated I'd been there for exactly five minutes. Josh and his executives had computer mainframe print-out paper sliced into smaller pieces and stapled as scratch pads, and would write responses in long hand directly onto incoming letters and memos and send them back to save time and paper. That's how he ran the business.

These executives are informed on every aspect of their company and are a windfall for analysts laden with extensive questions. But they have little patience for analysts and investors because their intense focus is on operating the firm. The chairman of Fiserv impressed me by knowing the name of every worker down on his loading dock. A member of EDS upper management picked up errant used paper hand towels on the men's room floor and placed them in the waste disposal. That's meticulous, rigorous detail. Generally, these are inside managers, with minimal outside public appearances. They can knock heads together, make things happen internally, build organizations, oversee, scrutinize, budget, track, and direct business operations. They are not much fun and have a short attention span, suffering no fools, but investors have little fear of a company faltering when such an executive is in charge.

Worrywarts Disguise Success Under a False Veil of Fear

This rare breed is highly competent, confident, even strident. It's a winning company that constantly downplays its success. These executives emphasize all the clouds and threats such as competition, pricing, new product uncertainties, industry changes, and unpredictable customer preferences. They also minimize earnings growth prospects and lowball their forecasts, the ultimate in managing expectations. The top executives of Microsoft are the poster boys of this style. At analyst meetings, they never fail to punctuate every presentation with the negative aspects, typically peripheral and often a stretch. Their earnings predictions each year are always conservative. We analysts become inured to this manner and give these cautious warnings little heed. IBM executives in halcyon years acted in a similar mode. Maybe when a company is so dominant and successful, it feels compelled to play down its fortune, embarrassed by the level of achievement, like big oil companies today. Investors need to realize that when management is overly conservative, it's normally a reassuring scenario.

Good 'Ole Boys Charm You While Deflecting Scrutiny

Amicable charm is a management style to be chary of. The nature of these executives is to be polite, and even enchanting. Because most analysts and institutional investors are from the east, New York and

Boston, they are unaccustomed to this demeanor and are easily swayed. Such sweet-talkeers have a good sense of humor and are entertaining. They are fun to be with for golf, wine, football, and other events, but this is a form of selling for them. Analysts and investors need to remain objective amidst this subtle social enticement. Good 'ole boys do not appreciate intense scrutiny or analytical skepticism. They usually dodge penetrating questions with a funny story or a humorous quip. Their attitude is "trust me." Although these executives want to appear as your friend, in actuality they are not.

A cool, powerful, macho, tobacco chewing CEO of an Atlanta-based firm offered me a beer when I entered his office for a routine analyst one-on-one meeting. I called him the Rhett Butler of the industry. He was my best friend when my investment opinion was bullish, but trash talked me to investors when I had a more cautious stance. It's easy to be seduced at first. This behavior is attractive and can breed initial trust. But watch out—it's dangerous. Investors can be taken in by nice guys who are just trying to curry favor with Wall Street.

Techy Geeks Who Know Their Stuff

Beware of persuasive talk by these technology nerds, usually founders of their companies. Their knowledge of tech products, software, and systems is deep, so they are compelling when discussing the technology. Biotech, pharmaceuticals, and other business based on science qualify here. Such executives confuse the issues with tech talk that is complex, way over your heads. Analysts and investors are nowhere near as steeped in understanding and do not even know the right questions to ask. If executives cannot present their product complexities in an understandable fashion, watch out. Investors should not be involved with companies they cannot grasp. It's the Warren Buffet principle. Geeky CEOs can intimidate investors into accepting their always auspicious explanations. These executives brag about their company's leading-edge expertise and attempt to snow investors with technical terms and commentary. But technologies and scientific disciplines change while founders stay pat. Geeks are confident, but are so narrowly focused that they miss broader issues, challenges, trends, and competitive shifts. Either avoid this type of company or gauge prospects broadly, not relying on the nerdy executive pitch.

Turnaround Artists Chase Windmills

Be suspect of any turnaround prospect. Temporary progress is usually a mirage; most measures to address problems are superficial and almost always too late. These executives are impressive, eloquent spokesmen, a breath of fresh air, professional, all-business, and give off an air of a savior with a plan. They are entertaining Harvard textbook studies, normally quite convincing, providing leadership in a time of company turmoil. Executives parachuted in to salvage failing companies are subject to glaring publicity and heavy Wall Street scrutiny, and are desperate to produce steady, quantifiable progress. Expectations are high; analysts and investors are eternally optimistic. Change artists have little to work with, as the company being resuscitated is usually a basket case. Michael Blumenthal (once U.S. Treasury Secretary) at Burroughs, Richard Brown at EDS, and Carly Fiorina at Hewlett-Packard are a few notable turnaround specialists that I have encountered. Their efforts were for the most part a failure.

These types are viewed as rescuers who arrived just in time. It is tempting to buy into their enthusiasm and confidence. Financial restructuring is usually their game, and that's easy. Cost cutting and stock buybacks are the norm, always the strategy. But such measures only buy time. The best these executives can achieve is to streamline operations and tee the company up for sale. The problem is their zealous attitude to prove to the world that they are the redeemer leads to the belief that they can actually revitalize the firm. They're ordinarily not interested in selling off the company quickly. The emphasis is on proving their turnaround artistry. In due course, the turnaround proves elusive and there are no willing acquirers ready to pay big bucks.

Promotional Hypesters Without Substance

Another common mold, these executives usually have a sales background and are expert at marketing. They mistakenly believe that the essence of their job description is selling. We analysts sit at meetings listening to their exciting presentations full of pizzazz. After 45 minutes, we look at our yellow sheet notepads and find no jottings— nothing material is uttered, all piffle. Frequently, they are off-putting.

A little hype goes a long way and it's commonly a cover up for lack of substance in a company. They treat analysts and investors like customers and the press, always pitching a positive spin, ever seeking an affirmative response, and sometimes resorting to promotive legerdemain. The curious thing is they believe their own blarney. Their press releases are stuffed with adjectives such as leading, enhanced, unique, significant, integrated, powerful, innovative, advanced, high-performance, and sophisticated. They talk lingo like mission-critical, strategic focus, go-forward plan, proactive, goal-oriented, and all the other commendatory buzzwords.

This management type is evangelistic. They never stop trying to convert the heathen. Larry Ellison at Oracle has this tendency. The chairman of Burroughs back in the 1970s was a scintillating salesman. The outlook was always bullish, trends continuously promising, the company could do no wrong. We could not ask any penetrating questions. He took that as an insult and just stuck to pushing his agenda. The company later skidded off the track and crashed. Most prominent leaders of the '90s Internet Bubble Era fit this mold, proselytizing their profitless new market pursuit as an inflection point and transformation, the new thing, eBusiness. Some of these were established titans who came from major corporations. They should have known better when they jumped onto the Internet bandwagon. These zealots were convincing, charismatic, and cool, but they almost all came to naught. Investors should be on the lookout for convincing salesmen whose story is hollow.

Exciting, Fast-Buck Smoothies Will Break Your Heart

This type of chairman or CEO is smooth as silk, the perfect host for a dinner party. He is enchanting, captivating, engaging, has a gift for gab, speaks with an air of confidence like an airline pilot, and is a good storyteller using colorful humor to punctuate points. Like the pilot in a storm, he always seems to have things under control. At least he gives off that impression. This demeanor can mislead naive analysts or investors. Business is never that steady or secure.

Slick, glib executives are good on stage and relish an audience. They regale customers, employees, industry groups, the press, and, more dangerously, analysts and investors. Responses to questions are spun in a glowing light, and negative issues are tempered or dismissed. Investors are treated like all other constituencies, cajoled, entertained, pitched, and made to feel good. The sell is subtle but constant. Wall Street is treated as just another type of client in the marketing effort. This executive is overconfident, arrogant, with a certain condescending attitude toward analysts, although these characteristics are extremely well concealed by the surface deportment. So when business turns sour and results tank, it's always a shock as there is never any indication of developing issues beforehand given the ongoing, incessant encouraging commentary. Investors need to be highly suspect of this polish because it's impossible to get an objective or informative view from this executive.

Executives In It for a Quick Hit

These breakneck opportunists typically show up on the scene with no industry background related to that of the current business. They sense a fleeting chance to get rich, start up or acquire entities to obtain a stake, and foist themselves off as a new wave executive in an emerging niche. Having little or no past history in the current sector, there is no record to review. The executive uses this to his or her advantage by claiming to be an original. Actions are aimed at immediate results, big contracts, notable high-profile hires, acquisitions, upfront deals—anything that will push the stock price higher. Watch their conduct as an indication of their intentions. Their remarks are always measured, business-like, and rational. But there is an underlying element of ambition, hurry-up, reaching, and opportunism. Their comments carry an undertone of bragging. They demean the competition and their managements.

In front of investors, these executives have a stridency, an attitude, and an arrogance, all of which transmit an air of confidence. It's easy to get swept up in the exhilaration of a fresh face leading a novel business with designs of making it big immediately. Growth forecasts are exceedingly high and unsustainable. This executive is often a winner initially, which leads analysts and investors to jump aboard the moon shot. It doesn't last long. This management does not build for the long run—it's like a zephyr—so underpinnings crumble. Attempting a surge strategy ends in a defeat. Expectations are too high. It's impossible to manage and control hyper-growth for long. It's a high-risk scheme that invariably leads to a debacle.

Ostriches Always Trail the Field

This is a low-profile, diffident, defensive, parochial, old-line management style. Executives do things the old-fashioned way, slow to move in new directions. They are probably Luddites and don't use email or carry around laptops. Management sees new trends late, is skeptical of anything different, is suspect of emerging forms of competition, and is satisfied with the status quo. It's like government bureaucracy. No enthusiasm. Creativity, flair, or originality is lacking. Although they are not susceptible to the mistakes of cutting-edge pioneers or aggressive, ambitious industry front-runners, the style leaves companies in a laggard industry position. Their rationale is that they are conservative, current-client focused, stable, low-risk, with robust finances. While there is some benefit to this approach, especially in a downturn or a slow period, this behavior results in lower profit margins and slower growth than the competitors. It's a dull management demeanor and produces a similarly bland corporate character, that of a straggler.

When analysts or investors meet with these executives, they are put to sleep. Analyst meetings and conference calls are boring affairs. These executives avoid the media. Their stocks have low PE multiple valuations. Investors will not be misled or bagged by such executives, and never be allowed any high expectations. Wall Street makes the mistake here of either being overly skeptical or wishfully thinking there will be a breakout, while generally the lackluster middle road is the accurate outlook.

Liars, Deceivers, and Manipulators

Despite the rage of regulators, legal pressures, governmental oversight, and '90s Bubble Era fall out, executives who mislead investors are ever lurking. Sometimes it's intentional, but it can also occur under the nose of a naive CEO, who perhaps chooses not to question how his top executives achieve their numbers. These cheaters never dream of being discovered. Some are charismatic, usually highly convincing, and the steady impressive results can be impossible for analysts and investors to discredit. A flourishing healthcare computer services firm I once covered, brought in a dynamic, impressive CEO to turn it around. He was a stellar performer for several years. The company became addicted to the immediate, upfront profit stimulus in signing software licenses. It turned out the books were cooked and guilty pleas followed. The perfectly smooth record had been falsified.

Another Internet service and software shooting star had hotshot technology gurus propounding its leading-edge industry expertise. At my conference, they were committed to conduct three breakout sessions, but bailed out for the golf course after the first period, leaving investors sitting in an empty room waiting for the second presentation. Two days later, their business scam was unmasked, and the stock crashed to almost nothing. So actually, the con artists who stood up some of my institutional investors that day did them a great favor, rather than doing all the meetings and continuing to lie about the prospects. A database software firm I once covered had a CEO who sported a gold chain necklace and gave me a certain sleazy feeling. I never trusted him or recommended the stock. He pleaded guilty to securities fraud in 2004, a felony charge of filing false statements with the SEC that inflated revenues, and was sentenced to serve a year in prison. Vigilance and scrutiny to determine the veracity of the income statement is not enough to avoid such crooks. It comes down to character judgment and that takes experience. Who do you trust? Dishonesty looms in many disguises.

Favorable Executive Traits

Once you are familiar with certain executive types, there is an array of traits to look for that are good indicators of management quality. Several reassuring executive characteristics suggest that a company is likely to have promising investment merit, key to any evaluation. Here are some management attributes that I seek when reviewing investment candidates.

Charisma, Leadership, Courage

Good leaders have a certain charisma that inspires employees and instills confidence in clients. Such executives are effective in moving companies ahead by their power of persuasion. I am impressed when employees have great respect and love for their leader. These executives must have the guts to do the right thing despite criticism, aggravation, and short-term stock impact.

Empowering Other Executives

Effective leaders attract, encourage, and empower other members of management. Less secure, power-hungry tyrants do not. Bill Gates trusts Steve Ballmer, and Larry Ellison at Oracle relied on Jeff Henley. The best leaders tolerate independence and strength among executives on their team.

Candor, Access

Executives gain credibility by being forthright, freely discussing negative cross currents and challenges. Access is critical, management must be open, available, and responsive to Wall Street and investors as opposed to being evasive or secretive.

Humble, Genuine

Company leaders should not be arrogant, no attitude or egos, minimal hype, and modest PR baloney. Firms in the Midwest, for example, seem to be more genuine. Executives should willingly admit mistakes and be willing to alter the course. No one's perfect or invincible.

Trust, Quality, Class

Management must be honorable, their comments reliable, their actions straightforward. They should act with class, not be litigious, display no vindictiveness, do nothing shady or sleazy. Investors need to be able to trust executives to the core.

Hands on, in Touch

Executives should be aware of what's occurring within the company at several levels and be in contact with the little people, not buffered by multiple management levels. Ross Perot was a master at this, chatting with his lowest-level associates in the elevator and in the cafeteria. John Chambers at Cisco engages all strata of employees.

Outgoing, Aggressive, Confident

I like to see these elements, and yes, they can co-exist with humility. Executives should not be shy, inward, or parochial. There needs to be a certain toughness, assertiveness, and conviction as long as there is the realization of vulnerability.

Creative, New Ideas

Leaders should be imaginative, with frequent new strategies, directions, and methods. They need to be flexible, resourceful, inventive, and unafraid to make changes. Transformation is invigorating, enhancing competitiveness.

Old-Fashioned Business Values

Management should be long-term oriented, use no temporal acts to boost immediate earnings, have a certain discipline, and avoid overpaying for acquisitions. They shouldn't have sumptuous headquarters or ostentatious perks. They should care about low-level employees and small clients.

Experience, Broad Backgrounds

Executives should have experience in a variety of disciplines such as manufacturing or operations, and backgrounds in other companies and market sectors. Too many executives have only sales or financial career paths.

Conservative, Understated

Executives shouldn't mix business with social styling and other over the top dress practice. I am bothered by flashy manners, extravagant events or meetings, and anything that substitutes superficial showmanship for substance. I am off-put by gold chain jewelry, monogrammed cuffs, overly chic designer shoes, or tony fashions.

Hard Working, Dedicated

Management should be as driven and consumed as analysts, and arrive before 7:30 AM and not depart until after 6 PM. They should travel on weekends and evenings, and lunch in the office. Their golf game better be marginal. I know a chairman who didn't do business breakfasts as they were too early. Not a good sign.

Undesirable Executive Demeanor

Certain undesirable conduct raises red flags and puts me on alert. Such demeanor is detrimental and usually indicates a problematic outlook for the company. Investors should be turned off by executives who display this type of comportment.

Dictator Surrounded by Yes-Men

CEOs or chairmen who are tyrannical dictators, sticking their noses in every detail, encircled by weak, wimpy yes-men, are likely to hit a brick wall. They can't be perfect, know everything, and always make correct decisions. They chase away real talent and effective leaders. The company outgrows them. Overly domineering autocrats create a vacuum in the management ranks.

Doing Too Much, Lacking Focus

Leaders should not be too diffused, travel too heavily, or make too many speeches or appearances. They can't work effectively on the road. Talk and rah-rah boosterism with employees and clients can ring hollow; often it's a substitute for the hard work of running the company. Executives need to concentrate and accomplish resolution on one or two big aspects, not try to do scores of tasks.

Kiddy Corps, New Age Commune, Love In

These are youthful founders and executives excessively exuberant, spiritual, reveling in community, treating business as a glorified love in, common in the '90s Internet Bubble Era. They refer to each other in cutesy terms: Bobby, Billy, and Johnny. The environment may be creative all right, zillions of ideas, but the atmosphere is like recess, just playing at business. Not a sound situation.

Hubris, Ego, Overconfidence

Executives should not be full of themselves. Too much of an attitude is a set-up for a fall. Ego is blinding. Roger Lowenstein of the *New York Times* said it best, "Hubris is not the worst crime—merely the one that guarantees the surest retribution." A superior peacock posture engenders hazardous behavior like overlooking competition or not listening to clients. Surprise setbacks are sure to follow.

Hype, Marketing, All Show

I am cautious when I see executives prominently featured in their own company advertising campaigns. Full-page ads and splashy airport billboards bother me. EDS ran a massive promotion and Super Bowl commercials, justifying the blitz as "air cover for the sales force." That chairman was later replaced when things swooned. Guess the aerial attack wasn't enough. Carly Fiorina featured herself in Hewlett-Packard ads and was later dismissed by the board. Beware of over-the-top hype and executive-centered publicity.

Lavish Digs, Perks, Packages

Read the proxy statement and annual report footnotes to note excessive executive pay packages and incentives. Stock appreciation rights, prodigious options, and $100 million paydays are a warning. The same for the fleet of corporate aircraft, ski lodges, and opulent headquarters.

Stock Price Fixation

Displaying the daily stock price at the corporate entrance check-in desk, employee cafeteria, and at analyst meetings connotes a short-term executive mindset. Management discussion of stock valuation is repulsive. They are managing the stock price instead of the company. Funny how when the share price is skyrocketing, executives take full credit for their brilliant vision, strategy, and execution—nothing to do with a bull market or the industry sector being in favor. For some reason, after the price plummets their stock prattle is muted, and the stock quote is no longer widely displayed around the office.

Private Life Demeanor, Reputation

I am put off by executives with a litany of ex-wives, messy public divorces, marriages to bimbos, visits to strip clubs, heavy drinking, active outside investment pursuits like real estate or private businesses, ostentatious McMansions and parties, sports cars, and profuse jet-setting. A study by two professors, as reported in the *Wall Street Journal*, found that "the bigger or pricier a CEO's house, the greater the risk of a lackluster stock performance." Showy sailboats, cars, planes, second homes, and bombshell women on their arms are bad signs of misplaced priorities. These executives are having too much fun and are not attentive enough to their business. Do you think Wall Street analysts are maybe totally jealous of such lifestyles? Of course, it's okay if executives play too much golf, especially with me.

Designer Suits, Fingernail Polish, Flamboyant Attire

Beware of executives appearing overly coiffed, like they just walked out of the salon, with fingernail polish, monograms, big rings, and fancy designer suits. Too much self-indulgence and emphasis on surface appearance, especially if self-glorifying, are a turn-off. These types lack substance and genuineness. Other affectations or cutesy personal marks like male ponytails and visible tattoos also bother me. They are attempts to portray images that I prefer to be demonstrated through actions and demeanor rather than as synthetic add-ons.

Trash Talk, Playing Favorites

Making negative aspersions about analysts or competing companies and products is a cover-up for internal corporate inadequacies. Any type of dissing is low class, and so is the practice of favoring analysts with positive opinions while freezing out those holding negative ratings. When executives criticize a negative research view, it indicates defensiveness. The analyst's insight was probably perspicacious, hitting close to home.

Overweight, Overindulging

Fat executives can reveal a certain lack of personal discipline that may translate to a similar absence of corporate control. I like to see executives who are lean and mean, healthy. Obesity can often parallel corporate overhead and indicate a lackadaisical style. I am similarly cautious of heavy smokers, drinkers, and womanizers.

Executive Actions Under Pressure Are Telling

Once you have executives pegged, it is helpful to observe their actions in times of crisis, when the company is under fire after a serious setback. These are the times to judge management character, to scrutinize their reactions, to see whether they take the proper, studied, rational, and calm course to rectify the situation. Frequently executives panic, behaving in a deleterious manner, making mistakes that compound the problems. Such damaging moves during troubled periods are like dousing the flames with fuel.

Even in Crisis Executives Are Eternal, Blind Optimists

Executives are too close to the firestorm. A stock I once covered, an early leader in the computer industry, announced a shocking business shortfall. The shares fell off a cliff. But the executives gave off an air that the problems were temporary, and things seemed to be under control. This message of minimal concern was accepted by traders and institutional investors. A big mistake. The disaster deepened, and the company collapsed and disappeared. It taught me to step back and assess such business setbacks with more perspective, using my own industry and company knowledge, and to pay scant attention to executive commentary during a crisis. It's easy amidst a disaster to be deceived by management into viewing the situation as not as bad as it appears on the surface. Canards flow freely. Executives take an insouciant attitude, which is misleading. The problem is almost always extensive, with more onerous implications than communicated by management. But it is too early for them to understand all the ramifications. Executives always believe everything will turn out all right.

When a company incurs a major problem and announces a surprising setback, executives usually go into spin control. They are subjective and defensive. In such a panic situation when a stock cracks badly, you as an investor, and for that matter analysts on the Street, are a better judge of the future outlook than what is being spewed from the suits. But seasoned analysts often have their own positive bias and vested interest. The individual investor can take a more arms-length view in a calmer manner and not be caught up in the turmoil. So, in this case, trust your own judgment of a panicked company.

Surprising the Street with Bombshell News

This error, often setting off some of the blunders described next, should be avoided in the first place. Favorable stunners are fine but negative announcements out of the blue impact credibility and cause investors to wonder what else might be wrong that is similarly uncovered. Executives should be forthrightly discussing issues, challenges, threats, and other vulnerabilities so that if any manifest into a serious jam, at least investors had warning of the possibility.

Assuming It's a Temporary Setback

Management always believes the current problem is short-term, one or two quarters in duration. But bad news comes in bunches. It usually gets worse and is always prolonged. Whether the issue is an order rate booking shortfall, a drop in profit, revenue slippage, a contract loss, or an adverse legal/regulatory decision, it is initially passed off as temporal or trifling. Corrective measures are tepid.

Blaming External, Uncontrollable Factors

To dodge culpability, outside causes beyond management's control are blamed—the economy, war, foreign currency, government, irrational competitor pricing, or a rival "buying" a contract. Setbacks and disappointing results may also be attributed to non-operational factors such as inferior forecasting, accounting, or reporting systems, rather than lack of competitiveness, weak markets, market share loss, or other more fundamental failings. Even analysts and the press are sometimes held responsible when companies falter. When Krispy Kreme Dough-nuts lowered its earnings guidance and indicated an SEC investigation in progress, it attributed slower sales to the low carbohydrate diet craze. Curious that Dunkin' Donuts incurred no such weakness. It's a natural tendency to deflect responsibility. If executives are trying to fool investors, they are only kidding themselves.

Inaccessible, Turning Insular, Out of Touch

In the eye of a storm, corporate leaders turn inward, wall themselves off and hide, and become inaccessible. Executives confer together but are out of touch with the outside world. They see the trees but miss the forest. It's calm on the inside while clients, suppliers, employees, and investors are roiled. Hiding from analysts, investors, and the press is a serious mistake.

Misplaced Confidence

When its stock plummets, a company takes umbrage, believing it's unwarranted, and will be short-lived. The down-turn is taken person-ally. A sizeable stock repurchase program is launched to indicate con-fidence in a recovery from the current predicament. This assurance is usually misplaced, the shares drop further, and the company ends up overpaying. Don't think for a minute that a buyback is a telling indica-tion of executive faith or sign that the stock is cheap. It's a desperate reach to feign conviction in a period of duress.

Firing the CFO or Middle Management, Keeping Inept Leaders

The buck stops at the top. But often when companies incur a major reversal, a business disappointment, they fire the chief financial officer as a scapegoat. And lower-level executives responsible for the problem are also terminated. Upper management should similarly be dismissed if a company is taking serious steps and not just shuffling the deck chairs. Higher-level executives are rarely held accountable. The cancer spreads because of denial or lack of enlightened direction at the top.

Frenzied Leaps, Strange Maneuvers

Companies in crisis act frantically, making last-ditch attempts to bail out of trouble, doing things like mega-acquisitions to stir up the pot. This diverts analyst and investor attention, casts a complicated, strategic new element into the mix, and buys time. They grab a gigantic contract at any price or give liberal payment terms to steal business, anything to boost immediate sales. Dramatic splashes in times of trouble never work.

Financial Schemes to Aid Earnings

Profits are temporarily boosted by stock buybacks, asset sales, capital gains on securities, write-offs, negative cash flow deals, and other balance sheet-related tactics. Stock repurchase plans are mere financial reengineering. They aid earnings and the stock price temporarily, but are a poor substitute for real growth. Financial transactions are transparent tricks to offset or obscure the operating problem. They merely underscore management despair, do not address the predicament, and are not resolutions.

Jaw-Boning Investors That Stock Overreaction Is Unwarranted

Stocks drop violently when bad news hits, stunning management. The first reaction is to insist that the price should not be so low. Executives address the wrong thing when speaking to investors, the stock price rather than the operating dilemma, criticizing Wall Street for overreacting. Management initially sees the issue as modest and passing. It does not perceive that things will further degenerate. But frequently a precipitous stock price swoon reflects more accurately the real situation than executives know.

Appraising management prowess is basic to determining a company's prospects. After all, these are the folks who will make or break your investment. You are relying on them to do the right thing, so you need to be a good judge of executive aptitude. Certain recurrent personality types and management styles can be readily identified. Other times, it's tough to draw a bead on what makes executives tick. It is all about character. In judging a company, you must gauge management first and foremost. You need to get it right, as in choosing a partner. It's vital. So carefully ponder the quality and effectiveness of a corporation's executive leaders before deciding to invest in the company's stock.

6

How Street Analysts Really Operate

Wall Street research began in 1934 with the seminal investment text *Security Analysis* by Graham and Dodd. Today, Street research entails quilting together information and understanding from a myriad of sources, and then drawing conclusions regarding the future outlook and potential for a stock. As a 32-year Wall Street analyst, my methods provide insight on how the Street operates and may serve as best practices for the individual investor. You might on occasion find yourself in a situation where you can conduct your own research similar to an analyst, maybe casually sitting next to an executive on a plane flight or at a social function. You certainly can tune into conference calls and view research reports or published company financials. If you emulate effective analyst procedures, you can gain valuable wisdom to make your own investment judgments.

Back in the day before analysts became so diluted and distracted, they actually did some decent, unbiased research. Recognizing how Street research has evolved and transformed will aid you in placing today's Street research in the proper context. My experiences as an analyst since 1971 are a good illustration of the road Wall Street stock research has traveled to arrive at its current state. And the present status isn't so hot. There are lessons still unlearned.

When Research Was Really Research

Research in the 1970s was pure, thoughtful, substantive, unbiased, and long-term. That's what we need to move back to. Investors should conduct their research in this manner, even though analysts and the Street can no longer operate this way. The 1970s was an era before desktop PCs. When I started, electronic calculators did not exist. Slide rules were the tool of the trade. At our boutique firm, we had one stock price quote machine for the entire research department and a single Dow Jones newswire service constantly printing out long reams of paper. There were no company conference calls. We often learned of quarterly earnings results by spotting them in the next day's newspaper. Analysts had to call the CFO to ascertain any numbers beyond reported revenue, net income, and earnings per share. There were no voicemails, fax machines, cell phones, pagers, or Blackberrys. After company meetings or at airports, we'd run for the payphones and use our AT&T calling cards. Travel agents wrote out by hand or typed airline tickets. There were no frequent flyer mileage programs. It was the Dark Ages.

Things moved slower, distractions were fewer, volatility modest. The only stock market TV program was the 30-minute Friday night Wall Street Week with Lou Rukeyser. Analysts had time to do real research. Because analysis was less quantitative, with no earnings models or spreadsheets, we tended to look more at business fundamentals and the bigger picture. My research reports had earnings model forecasts of a sort, but they were broken down annually not quarterly, and featured only five line items: revenue, profit margin, tax rate, share count, and earnings per share. Now that's simplicity. Reporters called infrequently, mainly from the *Wall Street Journal*. Television wasn't interested in analysts. Dialing clients took time, but because there was no voicemail and most calls resulted in busy signals, there were relatively few actual direct conversations per day. We just had more time to do pure research.

It was also a time of no research conflicts. All of the early quality level research was done by a few dozen boutique firms like the one I was at, Spencer Trask. One year in the early 1970s, it was ranked as the best research house by *BusinessWeek*, before the advent of the *Institutional Investor* rankings. Our research competitors were Donaldson Lufkin & Jenrette (DLJ), Smith Barney, Auerbach Pollack, F.S. Smithers, Rothchild, Cowen & Co., Faulkner, Dawkins, and the like. None of these did any degree of investment banking and most had precious little trading—nor did they cater to retail private clients. Profits flowed from institutions paying fixed commissions of $0.80 per share. Today, it's a penny a share. The big wire houses that dealt with retail individuals like Merrill Lynch, E.F. Hutton, Dean Witter, and Shearson did no in-depth research. Firms like Goldman Sachs, Morgan Stanley, and Salomon Brothers did investment banking and trading, no research. With essentially no investment banking influence, research was more impartial.

Investment opinions in the 1970s were longer range and deliberate, the same vane in which you should be approaching your own investments today. The investment community was on less of a treadmill than today. There was not as much emphasis on quarterly performance by the mutual fund industry. Daily trading volumes were at low levels, under 10 million shares a day on the NYSE, and there were no NASDAQ price updates—those stocks were "over the counter," and yesterday's prices were found in the Pink Sheets. Hedge funds had no influence, and quarterly corporate results were of only minor importance. Analysts not only had the time, but were expected to provide in-depth, thoughtful, and balanced reports and investment opinions. In my most bullish company reports, I still detailed all the negative risks. Institutional investors actually had time to read longer reports, unlike today. My Automatic Data and EDS reports contained lengthy discourse balancing positive and negative points, many pages of text assessing current operations and the outlook over the next couple years. The content had shelf life. It had to, since the report was distributed by U.S. mail and the reader probably got around to reviewing it a month later.

Analysts in those days were more professionally qualified. An analyst spent a decade or so to become seasoned. Serious career-minded, early stage analysts like me were persuaded to undertake the arduous three-year CFA program. The all-day exam in early June each year was an ordeal, just as it is today. A CFA designation is similar to a

CPA in accounting, passing the boards as an MD, or the bar exam for an attorney. It represents the utmost professional education for an analyst.

Research delved more deeply into business innards. Management access in those early years was easy, but had mixed consequences. It was a snap to obtain informal meetings with executives, to review the business and better understand the operations. This presented a stellar opportunity to develop the ability to judge management, their character, and effectiveness. The downside was that some executives, just like today, controlled and spun their stories in an attempt to sway analysts. There was not as much quantitative data or specific internal forecasts for corporations to divulge. Financials and detailed earnings models played a minor role. Discussions were broader, pertaining to operations, developments, and competition. We need to return to this approach.

Executives had more time to meet with investors and analysts. There were markedly fewer of us. Executives were not as inundated with demands on their time. Casual meeting opportunities abounded. We'd spend the morning seeing executives at NCR in Dayton, Ohio, and they'd join us in the afternoon at the top-ranked NCR South golf course. More executives were out there at the practice putting green over lunch than we'd spotted all morning at the headquarters. Analyst field trips to Nice on the French Riviera were punctuated by the heads of U.S. companies' European operations, slurping several glasses of Bordeaux during lunch while profusely spilling the beans.

Back in the U.S., IBM was so formal in white shirt attire and demeanor during that time period that puncturing its facade became a diversion for analysts. I remember the debut of its new PC that was to be distributed through Sears, a stunning new tactic for this computer mainframe juggernaut. During the analyst marketing presentation, a wag asked, "Will they be stacked on the floor next to lawn mowers or washing machines?." On another occasion, the chairman of a major technology firm made the keynote address to the computer services industry trade association. Computer services were an all-domestic business at that time. His staff prepared a formal speech on international trade, which he read off in 25 minutes. He then cut and ran, avoiding any questions. The whole show was exasperating, vastly missing the mark. I realized he was out of touch.

Beginning in the mid-1970s, Wall Street went through a massive consolidation and investment research began its metamorphosis. The days of research purity and objectivity were numbered. The profitable partnership environment on the Street collapsed quickly after May Day 1975. That was the end of fixed commissions, and they quickly shrunk to 5¢–10¢ a share. My first-year bonus of $2,000 melted to $100 four years later. Research boutiques folded and merged, no longer able to afford research without trading or investment banking revenues. That was the only way to pay for research going forward, sponsorship from the banking and trading departments. Commissions from big institutional investors like mutual funds underpinned the research budget. So analysts eventually became beholden to these forces.

Security Analysts Reach the Major Leagues

In the 1980s, Street research started to transmogrify, establishing the foundation of the current genre of security analysis. It dawned on big Wall Street brokerage firms that respected, authoritative, potent research could enhance their business almost across the board—institutional sales, trading, and investment banking. In only a few years, they bought all the leading analysts, enticing them away from smaller boutique brokerage firms. Morgan Stanley led the charge.

At the dawning of the modern era of research in the 1980s, a vigorous research revamp was afoot. Brokerage firm top managements were paying attention to research and expanding budgets there, and the new wave pushed the leading firms to the top research tier on the Street. We had respect, clout, and status within our firms. This was the early phase of analysts becoming important on Wall Street and to brokerage firms' bottom lines.

Research analysts steadily built teams and their coverage gravitated toward more specialization. The initial *Institutional Investor* poll in the early 1970s, ranking the best Street analysts, had less than 25 industry categories. By 2002, there were 77 sectors. That first year, the category encompassing essentially all high tech, the computer industry, components, and sundry other equipment was termed electronics, an incredibly broad area. During 1985–1995, my own coverage narrowed down from the computer industry to software/services and finally to just computer services. Even within the latter group, I concentrated on transaction processing and outsourcing, leaving consulting/professional services and a few other segments to my teammates.

So started the road that led to the spoiling of research. Once analysts were clearing real money, at around a half million annually, their egos inflated in line with the pay. Attitudes reflected our newly vital role within the business. Investment bankers, traders, and management started conferring with us. Analysts felt important. We were in demand by the press and seeing our names in print boosted our cachet. Now there were television interviews, further goosing our exulted status. Access to CEOs surged as they realized our sway on their stock was mounting. Company user groups, trade associations, and industry conferences all stepped up requests to have us speak at their forums.

As the heavyweight brokerage firms became research leaders, analysts still maintained a modicum of purity. Almost no bureaucratic encumbrances or compliance oversight meant analysts could shift opinion ratings on a dime, express views fairly freely, and had little investment banking inhibitions. They weren't bothered by having to be in contact with the traders. There were even some last vestiges of servicing and caring for the retail private client, the individual investor. I took the time to help found the Software/Services Analyst Group on Wall Street as its first president. This was all the buy- and sellside analysts tracking that industry.

It was still a period when analysts actually concentrated most of their efforts on conducting research rather than marketing. I made trips to Europe and Japan not to meet with investors, but rather to visit computer company managements, to survey the international competitive scene. During my first tour to Tokyo, the yen was king. Translating my car service tab from the airport to the Okura Hotel into dollars, I was sobered upon realizing the price was $500. Our travel agent had blundered and sent me off without a Visa, so I had to jam my meetings and speech to the Japan Society of Security Analysts into the maximum 72-hour transit limit. I was whisked through passport control with 30 minutes to spare, the Narita Airport officials doing double takes. They were suspicious of a transfer through the country, which normally took a few hours or maybe overnight, lasting three full days.

During this stage, probably reflecting my hyperactive nature, I got into long distance running. I ran cross country and the two-mile run on the track team in college, so when jogging first came into vogue, I knew that was a sport in which I could excel. Running was a stress release and a time when I could quietly ponder things, away from the maddening work setting and the two kiddies at home. And it quickly led to the Boston and New York marathons in 1980. On a cold day during the New York City Marathon, my running glove was snatched by a delinquent in Brooklyn. Running out of gas after the 20-mile mark in Harlem, the bystanders cajolingly cautioned, "You better not stop in this neighborhood!" At the finish of the New York Marathon that autumn, 3 hours and 35 minutes after the starting gun, I winged to Monterey, California for an annual high-tech conference, flaunting my medal prominently around my neck at all the meetings. Rupturing my Achilles tendon the next year, I saw my racing days come to an end. The arduous racing and hours spent training were indicative of the disciplined, hardworking, and patient approach to my career.

Salomon Brothers in the early 1980s spawned some notable industry leaders. Lewis Ranieri as the pioneer of mortgage-backed securities created a massive new market. He was a wild, pen-chewing, driven powerhouse. John Meriwether was lurking in fixed income. Later he spawned Long-Term Capital Management with other industry luminaries. Before long, it came a cropper and almost dragged the entire market under, amidst notorious controversy. There were other stalwarts like Henry Kaufman and Michael Bloomberg.

While covering EDS at that time, I sensed something strange was afoot there. Newspapers were reporting that two EDS managers overseeing its contracts in Iran had been taken hostage in the revolution against the Shah. EDS executives in Dallas were hushed and distracted. Perot was orchestrating an amazing commando raid led by Bull Simons, a U.S. Green Beret Colonel in Vietnam who had previously led a rescue attempt outside Hanoi. EDS took matters into its own hands, since the State Department was of no help. It spared no expense, and at one point, Ross Perot himself, in disguise, wandered into the Tehran prison to surreptitiously contact his two captives. The tale is an enthralling real-life saga of prison overthrow, close calls with junta leaders, suitcases stuffed with bribe money, overland jeep chases, and storming through border guards without passports. Ken Follett depicts this riveting episode in his book, *On the Wings of Eagles*.

A few years later, the General Motors acquisition of EDS was a turning point in my career. Salomon was a trading firm and also a major investment banking force. Research was viewed as a back office support function, and though managed somewhat autonomously from banking, we analysts were second-class citizens. This dawned on me when I was told that my total annual compensation including bonus for 1984 would be unchanged from the prior year, despite my key role in the GM deal that generated $7 million in fees to the firm, a gargantuan sum in those years. I grasped that, regardless of my contributions, the prospect to make it big as an analyst at Salomon was limited.

The story of the GM-EDS deal is captivating as told in Doron Levin's book, *Irreconcilable Differences*. I was part of the drama. To further the banking relationship with General Motors, noting its newfound inclination to diversify, a Salomon banker put together a list of five acquisition ideas. GM's treasurer Courtney Jones jumped at the EDS suggestion. An offer was made to Ross Perot that got his attention: $1 billion to him personally in realizable net worth. That was real money in those days. Ross sold EDS, obtained a fabulous no-risk convertible security in addition to cash, and then proceeded to maintain full operational control of the EDS subsidiary. He stopped the GM auditors at his Dallas headquarters gates, refused to open his books, and proceeded as if the company had never been acquired. The battle with GM's chairman Roger Smith was joined.

EDS's relationship with GM was combative; the forced surgical EDS implant was being rejected by the GM bureaucracy. Despite the negative impact of this culture clash, the colossal new computer processing business from GM tripled the size of EDS, enhancing its revenues and earnings. As the leading Street analyst on the stock at a firm playing a lead investment banking role doing follow-on stock offerings, I had to walk a tight rope. This was an early hint of research conflicts with investment banking that was to manifest in the 1990s.

Within a couple years, Perot, a GM board member, was excoriating Smith publicly, "Until we nuke the GM system, we'll never tap the full potential...." And by the end of 1986, Ross and his key management compatriots got bought out of their $750 million convertible securities early and walked dazed but lucratively out the heavily guarded EDS campus barricade for good.

When my son was 10 years old and had a passion for railroad trains, we took off on EDS's plane with Paul Chiapparone, a senior executive (and incidentally, one of the two EDS hostages sprung in the Iranian raid) to tour GM's locomotive engine manufacturing plant in Canada. We operated a newly minted diesel railroad engine on the test track, Justin got 6 turns in the engineer's seat, I could barely nudge him out for one go at the controls. He flew co-pilot on the EDS jet heading back home to New York. Not a bad day for a 10 year old.

Digging for Skeletons and Pumping Executives

Since the 1980s, acting as an investigative reporter has been key to research. This means digging out information about companies that executives are unwilling to disclose. Usually it's negative. They give out voluntarily only the glowing side of their story, rarely divulging detailed operating data broken down by division or group, and never the adverse issues. Analysts scramble to glean more in-depth understanding. Sometimes this necessitates some honest thievery. Analysts are always on the lookout for fat three-inch thick company binders for internal use only, sitting in an airport lounge or hotel conference room, containing all the statistics on dozens of divisions and tons of other facts and information, like corporate clients. This gives them a fix on aspects that executives would never willingly divulge.

Creative insight and clever probing to some degree has always been a hallmark of good research. In the 1970s and 1980s, the only way to discover what was happening inside a particular company I covered was on a piece-meal basis from lower-level employees. At my two-day public speaking course in uptown New York, I was startled to see that most of the other participants were junior sales persons from that firm. All of their five-minute practice speeches pertained to current sales issues and challenges. Keeping my identity under wraps, I took copious notes and zipped my lips. It was an incredibly insightful inside assessment—a revealing information dump. Always be aware of and listen to people around you.

I also recall a plane flight where a Computer Associates salesman told me all the games and gimmicks that the software company practiced to create a revenue mirage, what I had long suspected but had difficulty pinning down. I never trusted them again. Eventually management was charged by the SEC for fraudulent accounting and pleaded guilty to a federal indictment. Some of the best information sources are middle-level executives who banter like jocks in a locker room. The analyst's role is to put this valuable input in the proper context, weighing it with other public information, realizing it may be myopic, isolated, or unimportant. Or it may generate sensitive questions to lob at top executives. Their reaction can be telling, as broaching these skeletons usually catches them off guard. Executives strive mightily to prevent outside investors and analysts from viewing internal dirty laundry. While individual investors are unlikely to have this opportunity, they certainly can listen to management reactions to analyst questions on conference calls or in press interviews.

Investors need to be prepared to weigh properly what they hear from executives. Direct incidental contact and information can be a unique source of research, but you need to do your homework. Never take an isolated conversation as the sole reason to make an investment. The company must check out on numerous other counts. If you have a close executive relationship, say your neighbor or old school friend, this begins to flirt with inside information. And any look that's too deep into the inner workings of a company can produce the affect of being blinded by the trees rather than seeing the whole forest. Another risk is that close executive relationships may aid understanding but often cause a favorable bias. Analysts on Wall Street invariably have a certain degree of friendship with corporate executives that presents an invaluable source of information and access, but it is a two-edged sword. The trade-off is a human tendency toward preferential treatment.

An organization that I am still actively involved in, the Business Executives for National Security, once presented a tangential opportunity for me to schmooze with CEOs. The chairman, Josh Weston of

Automatic Data Processing, invited me to join an Air Force tanker refueling mission en route from New York, to the Strategic Air Command (SAC) base in Nebraska. That renewed my tie with the military, having endured three years aboard a Navy LST ship out of Norfolk as an operations officer in the mid-1960s. On subsequent outings like aircraft carrier night flight operations, nuclear submarine dives, Army tank battles, and an F-16 flight, I bonded with other company chairmen. I had a love-in with one CEO who had earlier bad-mouthed me to other analysts. There's nothing like being strapped in a four-way harness in a seat facing backwards on a Navy transport plane, violently hitting the deck and catapult wires, while landing on an aircraft carrier, to stir up a conversation with the executives on board. More recently, I've been to Iraq and Afghanistan with this outfit. Camaraderie stems naturally when confined on a military venture.

Golfing was another good venue to build personal relationships with executives. After kidding around for 4½, hours, competing for whopping $5 or $10 stakes, and downing a couple beers, you become friends. After that, it's personal. So when I called the CEO, he was ready to chatter, mostly about golf, but that always gave me an opening to broach business topics. The chairman of a company I covered introduced me to Arnold Palmer before we contested a round at Bay Hill. And he also hosted me at the 2000 Masters golf tournament in Augusta. Such camaraderie diminishes the normal disclosure barriers between executives and analysts. I was not particularly privy to sensitive inside information, but I did get better vibes, leanings, and a sense of direction on key issues.

Another time, one of that firm's biggest contracts was about to expire and Wall Street was uncertain if that client would be re-signed. Somewhere along the 18 holes I spent with a member of management at my California Golf Club, I gathered the impression that a successful re-negotiation was imminent. No details. But it was enough to assure me. I took that stance, and it was validated shortly thereafter. It's not always golf. Things like the Atlanta Olympics in 1996 where I attended a couple events with another company's executives similarly helped in establishing close social relationships. When that same firm shocked the Street that autumn with news of an earnings shortfall, I knew which members of management I could trust to get the straight scoop.

Talking to executives is an art. As an investor, you must decide if what you hear makes sense. Does it stack up? Does it ring true? Analysts act as consultants with a thorough understanding of the industry, competitors, users, and trends. And they have an in-depth grasp of a company's business, past record, issues, and management. So we should be qualified to gauge executives' remarks. Still, it's not easy. We can get fooled. In any casual conversation you might have with executives or opportunities such as tapping into conference calls, you need to be on guard. Sometimes you can discern reality by observing their reaction to bold questions. Analysts are eternally cast in a skeptical vein. Because their opinions are mostly approving, contrary surprises are their biggest fear and worst nightmare. So analysts constantly probe for weaknesses.

Executive discussion is the chief basis for an analyst's understanding of a company's business and trends. Regulation Fair Disclosure (Reg FD) requires full company disclosure to the public, all at the same time, of any material information that could influence the stock price. This new requirement has had the effect of muzzling executives in the last few years. They are now unable to give any selective forecasts, guidance, or broad indications of expected future progress. Still, things dribble out in phone conversations. Street insider awareness is enhanced with specific questions usually aimed at the CFO or head of investor relations (IR). Most analysts have direct access to these two company representatives. It is rarer to have as easy an entrée to the chairman or CEO. The advantages in being an analyst for so long were my age and industry standing. Several chairmen viewed me as a peer, which aided my reception. I played golf, dined at the homes, and attended the symphony with these company leaders, all occasions for serious bonding. Younger analysts had no such relationship.

Analysts must distinguish the truth from all the spin control, hype, rationalization, and blather. Close rapport helps. As friends of a sort, executives are less likely to grossly mislead us. They cannot give us a scoop, but they can lead us down the right path. When a software firm launched an unfriendly takeover of a services company I followed, the latter's chairman obliquely indicated to me in a surprisingly firm manner that his defense would prevail. That's all I needed to hear, no specifics. I knew I could trust him since our relationship was on a friendship basis, things like a weekend on the links at Turnberry, Scotland. So I staunchly put forth this conclusion. It proved to be absolutely correct.

There are many facets to management contact. If we take no notes, they speak more freely. Still, most analysts scribble frantically. Sticking to important, broad topics is key with a chairman. You can't expect an executive at that level to know the capital spending budget for next year or the nuances of percentage completion accounting. CFOs are the source for financial matters. Don't presume they can help on aspects like products, manufacturing, or research and development. Rapid response is another measure. Leading analysts who have the most influence on a stock get such treatment. So when a callback lags, our antennas send an alert warning or signal that something major is pending, about to be announced. I once downgraded my opinion at the end of a quarter on a company that was unresponsive in this manner. Usually it was quick to call back. I read a pending earnings shortfall disclosure into this uncharacteristic pause, forewarned investors, and the stock price sank. A mistake. Everything was fine, but the company never failed to return my calls promptly after that.

Reading Executive Body English at Meetings and On Conference Calls

Executive interaction is in its most concentrated form at the meetings companies hold to brief Wall Street institutional holders and security analysts. These are usually annual affairs lasting from three hours to one and a half days. Executives are paraded onto the podium, audio-visuals are flashed on the screen, bulky notebooks contain copies of all the slides. We scrawl voluminous notes and ask endless questions. But the best input is during informal coffee breaks. On stage, the remarks are planned, canned, always with an optimistic spin. Companies spend hours talking but saying nothing; 99% of the commentary is mellifluent hype. Although important disclosures are a rarity, it's still imperative we attend. Analysts can detect an overall tone, read body English, sense any hesitancy, observe strident confidence, get an impression of executives, and even see the attitudes of investors in the audience. There is usually a momentary reaction that moves the stock that day in concert with the tenor of the session.

Normally these meetings are mundane, even tedious. But not always. Once, at the yearly Microsoft gathering in Seattle, the scheduled meeting was shifted following a bomb scare to a convention hall near the Navy piers. But Bill Gates had a better idea to corral the 250 Street professionals. Within a couple hours, he had reconnoitered with the commanding officer of an aircraft carrier tied up nearby. Even the U.S. Navy made way for Bill Gates. Chairs and audio-visual equipment were arranged on the hangar deck, and all the analysts calmly embarked, enthralled by the imposing military venue. We never determined whether it was all a set-up or if it was truly spontaneous.

EDS at one point held a Texas barbeque on its ranch land outside Dallas and gave the gathering helicopter rides. On another occasion, I observed a stern, proud executive at a trade association meeting take two steps backward from a raised lectern and crash three feet down into a heap. Disappearing from view, he whimpered "I think I'm alright." Afterwards, he pleaded with me to keep the matter silent from his fellow executives back in the home office, lest he become a laughing stock.

The content of meetings with the Street is normally predictable; rarely are there any newsy or dramatic developments. Microsoft always low-balls the outlook, reducing expectations. Analysts disregard it. Sometimes, though, forecasts can be alarming. Computer Sciences once put forward tepid revenue guidance, the shares were creamed, and it was the first indication of a several-year industry-wide downturn in consulting and outsourcing. EDS once astounded a group with the bullish revelation that it was bidding on a contract some 25 times the size of any previous deal. That started a 16-year run in the stock. These are exceptions.

Conference calls are good background information, saving management time from getting on the horn with countless analysts and institutional portfolio managers. These conference calls take research to yet another level of detail. In the years prior to the orchestrated group calls, analysts chatted with executives for 20 minutes max to better understand the just-reported results. Now everyone can listen in for an hour or more.

On the downside, all parties monitoring these calls get the same spoon-fed executive hogwash and all Street research reports reflect this similar information—another nail in the coffin of distinctive, original, creative research analysis. The Street is like reporters, parroting executive explanations, its role of an objective, reasoned research source diminished. Because the Street largely just churns out what is said on the call, you don't even need to read the reports if you listen in on the call.

Conference calls are usually connected with news flashes or press releases. Reacting to late-breaking, impact news on companies is a recurring investor challenge. Events like earnings shortfall pre-announcements, contract awards or losses, acquisitions, and management changes often require an investor to make a judgment. The immediate impression is usually the correct one under such pressured conditions. This is where a certain feel comes into play. Often you must do a fair amount of guessing based on background understanding. Your knowledge of the companies you own is the key to putting most breaking announcements in the proper context. The difficulty is to avoid an emotional reaction. Make a detached, impartial conclusion when engulfed in a firestorm. A natural tendency is to bend a new development to fit your ongoing investment position, belittling the consequence if it runs counter to your stance. Don't be blinded by unconditional faith. Although normally the best course is to sit tight until calm is restored and a reasoned opinion can be reached, once in a while the turn of events is a dramatic enough catalyst, a Black Swan event, to shift your investment view. This should be the exception, but never be oblivious to the possibility that all of a sudden it's a whole new ballgame.

Conducting an annual industry conference is another essential element in Street research. Most brokerage firms hold these forums, featuring the industry sector company executives. Competition to draw investors is fierce. My strategy was to be the first one of the year, so we scheduled our conference in early January, to one-up my counterpart rival analysts. My format was also unique, all casual Q&A breakout sessions, no dreary canned stage presentations. And we held these events offsite in plush Florida resorts like the Ritz-Carlton on Key Biscayne. Our audience was captive for 2½ days compared to a New York location, where investors pick off a couple meetings and return to their offices. We always teed up colorful industry-related characters, H. Ross Perot, a NASA astronaut, and the like, to entertain at intriguing dinner sites like museums or mansions. Our annual shindigs grew to become the best annual conference in the sector. My decades of rapport with the companies in the industry brought out more senior executives, chairmen, and CEOs than any of my competitors' gatherings.

Individual investors are not invited to these shindigs. And little surprising news or major developments are ever disclosed. In this era of full disclosure, executives are muzzled, confined to PR pabulum, and if there is any real company news, it's put out in a press release. There's only one sellside brokerage analyst at such a conference—the one giving it. And he's consumed with running the show. So don't expect much research comment from his firm other than pro forma BS. These conferences are basically a marketing ploy to butter up institutional investor clients and gain brownie points with executives. If there's any material effect on the stock of the companies presenting, it stems from the major institutions in attendance deciding to buy a stock after hearing the story. This can push up the price for a short time.

The Numbers Sing But Keep Them in Perspective

Numbers, details, and data are boring, but vital, in making investment choices. Elaborate, extensive earnings models have become a dominating aspect of research. These are multiple page columns and rows of quantified data. They start at the top with sales and revenues, filtering all the way down to earnings per share, but also extending way beyond that to cash flow statements, balance sheets, and other data like order rate bookings. Models are built sedulously, mostly by junior analysts.

My philosophy has always been that the numbers sing. Models are the ultimate in diving down into minute quantitative levels of the income statement. Executives are compelled to aid the Street in the forecasting aspect when analysts develop and update the models. The end product is a measuring tool to monitor scores of different financial elements each quarter as companies report results. They virtually tell the whole story of the health of a company. By analyzing recent financial patterns and trends, facilitated with detailed models, we acquire a reasonable grasp on potential future results. The only problem

I had was that I never knew how to build such a model on a personal computer. I entered Wall Street way before the PC era, never used computers in school, and despite close brushes with technology somehow managed to remain a Luddite. My kids, of course, are the opposite. At a press conference in the 1980s where I spoke about my book on the computer industry, my daughter Laurel, just starting elementary school, was asked if she was learning to use computers in school. She quipped, "No, we're just programming in Basic!"

Models have altered the research landscape. Corporate financials are under massive scrutiny, on myriad degrees of specificity. Earnings spreadsheets have led to an environment where analysts are harder to please, because each quarter there are invariably certain items in the results that come in wide of the mark, causing questions and forcing corporate executives to be defensive. The Street can always find fault somewhere in the quarterly income and cash flow statements or balance sheet. This is probably healthy, though the inherent skepticism was temporarily set aside in the tidal wave of euphoric cheerleading in the 1990s.

That said, be dubious of research that overly weighs models in the analysis. Concentrate on the broader scenario and factors shaping the outlook. Do not be entangled in exhaustive earnings model minutiae. Even professional Street portfolio managers do not have the time or skills to get mired in such mathematical detail. Individual investors can never be expected to grapple with these quantitative monsters. Analysts have become so bogged down in the numbers that they are less observant of the big picture, prompting a tendency to miss industry inflection points or critical corporate crossroads.

The prominence of models has detracted and displaced the ancient art of undertaking original investigative legwork, talking to customers, checking with former executives, spending time with competitors, or meeting with outside experts. This unbalanced, highly quantified, stay in the office, model-driven mathematical research approach is like a medical laboratory test facility. A patient needs the balance of experience, awareness, and bigger picture knowledge from a general practitioner M.D. for proper overall diagnosis rather than exclusive dependence on the lab results and statistics. Models are altered constantly, tend to be based on consensus with little "forecastive" value added, and are of limited use to investors and portfolio managers. Don't think detailed financial metrics suggest precise accuracy, but don't neglect this quantitative aspect either. Just put it in the proper perspective.

Regardless of models, street research is still not focused enough on financial and accounting matters. Analysts occasionally become enamored with a new technology, drug, or other promising prospect that is all futures. There is no substitute for earnings, cash flow, and strong finances. If any of these are lacking, it is a highly speculative stock. If earnings are problematic or negligible, or there is negative cash flow, or a notably debt leveraged balance sheet, it sounds an alarm bell. When these factors are downplayed or explained away with mitigating circumstances, don't buy into the thesis. Equity analysts' understanding of financials is modest compared to credit and fixed income analysts. Most stock research fails to delve deeply into the latter disciplines—balance sheets, cash flow, working capital, liquidity, and accounting and financial disclosure practices. Street research needs to intensely probe companies experiencing consistent negative cash flow, showing suspiciously bulging unbilled revenues or aberrant shifts in working capital, as would a fixed income analyst. The main elements of the balance sheet and cash flow statements must be analyzed and highlighted more specifically. More omens would surface earlier by emphasizing this, as compared to the current accent on earnings and revenue growth prospects.

Don't think Street earnings estimates connote any real degree of predictability. Precise earnings forecasts imply a ridiculous level of accuracy and mislead investors. Estimates change several times throughout the year. Companies are under artificial demands to meet or exceed a specific quarterly earnings expectation. Stock price volatility is exacerbated by quarterly results that vary by as little as 1¢ from a pinpoint Street consensus expectation. Estimates, both annual and quarterly, should be in ranges to properly portray their inexactness, leaving room for movement.

Research Buttresses Investment Banking in '90s Bubble Era

By the 1990s, the value of analysts and their enhanced rapport with CEOs of companies they tracked began to be recognized by investment bankers. Close analyst associations with executive leaders of companies under coverage were becoming meaningful in brokerage firm investment banking relationships. Commonly the analyst had better access to the chairman or CEO than the banker. That was important in winning a banking assignment. Although analysts actively participated in banking deals in the late 1980s and early 1990s, they were not beholden—no biased entrapment yet. Investment banking was not yet an outsized, massive contributor to brokerage firm bottom lines compared to the coming '90s Bubble Era. Its role was still balanced, and analyst research maintained some measure of autonomy. Despite the intensified analyst teaming with investment bankers to obtain deals and execute offerings, they were still reasonably objective in their research opinions even on investment banking clients.

"It was the best of times, it was the worst of times." With regard to analysts and research, Dickens characterization applies in spades to the '90s Bubble Era. The excesses, influences, biases, and distortions in that astonishing late 1990s bull market were like the 1920s. Professionalism suffered. It was analysts gone wild; the ruination of credible research. I was a 25-year veteran at the time and old-fashioned enough to just not get it. The more professional, rational analysts like me were called relics. It felt good to be back in style later, once the bottom fell out of the Internet stocks.

That incredible period was bountiful for an extremely wide spectrum of people. Virtually every party involved endorsed and blessed the wildly bullish times, from Fed Chairman Greenspan to the Chairman of the SEC, individuals to corporate CEOs, venture capitalists to analysts, the press to governments, car dealers to real estate agents. My airport taxi driver bragged about his wife sitting at home day trading, actually piling up some material capital gains, believing it was a one-way street. Governments, corporate pension funds, and charity endowments saw tax receipts, surpluses, and portfolios bulge. The disproportionate federal and state tax collections stemmed mainly from the wave of capital gains and stock options exercised. They all seemed to think it was the result of their own astute policies and, even more incredulously, that it was permanent.

It even dawned on my daughter that there was money to be made in stocks. She was coming of age, just entering college, and I salted a few stocks into her own brokerage account. The stocks climbed, she noticed, and all of a sudden she had more regard for my business. I told her that stock price appreciation was called capital gains. Her retort was, "Dad, I like capital gains! Can you give me more of them?" Later I attempted to entice this college graduate, who had majored in archeology and art history, to a career on Wall Street. Fat chance. I sat her down for an afternoon at our sales and trading desk in San Francisco. Anticipating that this experience would peak an emerging interest in the investment field, I inquired of her reaction. She was underwhelmed and blurted "Those guys up there are cute!" This woman was headed in a totally different direction.

The roar from Wall Street produced stellar buoyancy in the economy, soaring real estate prices, and abundant jobs with Internet start-ups for kids just out of college. Street professionals basked in influence and compensation, and that extended to venture capitalists, fund managers, bankers, and treasurers. All these groups benefited regardless of, or maybe because of, the litany of improper Street practices that were later uncovered.

In research, budgets were flush, almost unlimited, analysts had the freedom to build out their teams. Firms added associates to work for other analysts in the group, research assistants with college degrees. Office spaces bulged out. With such resources, teams produced lengthy tomes; industry studies and reports amounting to hundreds of pages that looked like phonebooks. Quarterly industry reviews proliferated; user surveys mushroomed. Investors and portfolio managers never had time to pour through all this tedious detail, but corporations and executives in those industries were pleased to have these industry research publications float in over the transom for free. The thicker the magnum opus, the more our expertise shined, like a college term paper.

Securities analysts and research were vastly altered during this euphoric period. Analysts became kings, gained stunning clout, their power and influence sending stocks into the stratosphere. As public awareness surged, analyst stature reached unimagined heights, rivaling Hollywood celebrities. Crazed star-struck new generation analysts—actually "cheerleaders"—were awarded 3-year guaranteed contracts. Bonuses followed suit. On marketing trips instead of one-on-one appointments, meeting rooms swelled with a dozen or more portfolio managers. Analysts had the ear of CEOs, and obtained instant access to top management of the companies under coverage, red carpet treatment, a rarified entrée. They created revenues for their firms and wealth for investors. Investment recommendations and price targets ignited stock prices. Stock Buy ratings turned out to be "fabulous ideas," surging upwards. *Institutional Investor* magazine has an annual feature profiling home run hitters, an analyst whose Buy opinion that typically had moved up 100% or 200%. In the late 1990s it took stock surges of more than 1000% for a stock idea to make that list.

The 1990s has many parallels, such as the mid-1800s U.S. railroad proliferation, which were the growth stocks of that era. They sprung up in months, right-of-ways as short as a few miles, went public quickly, and were chased by investors at a feverish clip. Almost all of them were soon acquired for a few cents on the dollar or went bankrupt. I have more than a hundred old railroad stock certificates from that period, a fraction of the thousands of publicly-traded names during that time. Internet companies repeated this pattern in the late 1990s.

Another historical guidepost is the incredible 1980s Japanese stock market explosion when many sectors, such as textiles and shipping, saw price-to-earnings multiple valuation levels top 100x. Rationale emerged to justify these radical heights, such as understated earnings, cross shareholdings, and world economic leadership. And, similar to the U.S. Internet bubble, Japanese investors rewarded market share expansion rather than profit growth. Real estate prices in Japan leaped off the charts, and the Japanese chased trophy properties around the world like Pebble Beach and Rockefeller Center. The stock most typifying that bubble was Nippon Telephone and Telegraph (NTT). Its shares sold at a price/earnings multiple of 200x and it reached 3 million yen before capitulating 80% to 500,000 yen in the early 1990s. And Japan's Nikkei index rolled over from 40,000 to 15,000 in the same timeframe.

The 1920s was the ultimate period of euphoria when greed was a contagion. Bubbles are characterized by John Rubino, author of *Main Street, Not Wall Street*, as most likely when there emerges new technologies, new business practices, or new leading companies. In the Roaring '20s, the company that personified this profile was Radio Corporation of American (RCA). Its stock price soared from under $10 to $100 during that period, and back to below $10 in the 1930s. In the 1920s pre-existing standards of value such as net asset value or dividend yield were tossed out. There was a proliferation of automobile, telephone, and aircraft manufacturers, the new technologies of that era. The 1990's Internet explosion also resulted in thousands of IPOs, newly public companies with wildly excessive valuations. They were even more profuse as there were essentially no capital requirements compared to the manufacturers of the 1920s. Key observers at the time termed the 1920s as an era of limitless prosperity. Market experts like an influential Yale economist talked about the market reaching a "permanently high plateau." In the recent epoch there were books forecasting the Dow at 36,000. Both eras evoked a crowd mania in terms of investor sentiment, in the 1920s shoeshine boys were plunging into the market, in the 1990s waiters were doing day trading.

The '90s Bubble Era rewarded corporate market share gains and intriguing conceptual business plans rather than profit improvement. Traditional valuation measures like price-to-earnings (PE) ratios were discarded in favor of imagined future discounted cash flows. That's because PEs became infinite for the plethora of Internet start-ups that were running red ink. In early 2000, Yahoo!'s market value was $105 billion, greater than the combined automobile and auto parts industries! Laws of economics were temporarily suspended, profits were not necessary, the key was the concept, market share, sales, futures, or any number of enticing mirages. The S&P 500 Index tripled in 5 years, in the roaring 1920s bull market the Dow Jones Industrial Average quadrupled in six years during 1923-1929. PE multiples peaked at 46.5x on reported earnings in December 2001. The historical 25 year norm is around 15x.

The shocking stock market excesses of the 1920s decade-long bull run ended in the massive collapse during the 1930s and were the catalyst behind radical stock market reform measures under Joseph P. Kennedy and the new, Roosevelt created, SEC. It took a decade to offset the 1920s excesses and install necessary reforms. Some 25 years passed before the stock market recovered, by 1954, to the previous highs of 1929.

Internet Euphoria Perverts Street Research

In the '90s Bubble Era, derisively known as the "dot-con" era, companies with hundreds of millions of venture capital to blow and no prospect of ever earning a profit, became the "New Economy." It was the rise of the great American money machine called the new paradigm. Internet start-ups went public and saw their stocks reach triple figures. The magazine of choice was *Red Herring*, pertaining to Internet and tech IPOs, with over 300 workers and circulation of 275,000. The mutual fund managers wanted "the new stuff," such as Priceline.com. It surged to $162. Computer services companies that I covered, like EDS and First Data, with a fast revamp of their PowerPoint presentations and a change in logo, became eCommerce B-to-B eBusinesses because it helped their stock prices.

Green analysts were abundant during the '90s Bubble Era and research quality reflected their immaturity. Bull market babies, who became Wall Street analysts amidst the vortex of a flourishing economy and a soaring stock market, hardly had the proper awareness of a potential downturn or any appreciation of its possible impact. Reckless analysts and investors were all foolish. They propounded the theory that the old rules didn't apply anymore; that elephants could fly. And they did, but not for long. The Internet boom/bust stories are legend. It was all about absurd expectations, a chimera. Heed the lesson.

eToys peaked at $84 and sunk to zero. Webvan launched its IPO at $35, its trucks were seen scurrying all over San Francisco and a few other cities, $1.2 billion in capital was burned. A billion here a billion there—really just play money at the time. And then oblivion. Pets.com went public a month before the March 2000 market climax, peaking at $14. By later that year, it announced plans to liquidate and it shut down. Mp3.com shot up to $105, a market value of $5.6 billion, before its demise. Dr. Koop.com top ticked at $45, a market cap of more than $1 billion, before capitulating to nothing and pulling the plug at the end of 2001. Theglobe.com went public in late 1998, roaring ahead 60% its first trading day, to close at over $63. Two and a half years later, it was de-listed from NASDAQ and traded for 16¢. It wasn't only Internet names. Some shooting stars were in telecom network equipment. Redback Networks was a wonder, a public offering in 1999, the stock reaching its apex of $191 in March 2000, Chapter 11 in late 2003, the shares worth a few cents. Losses over its short lifespan amounted to $5.4 billion, which was serious red ink for a tiny firm whose revenues never surpassed $278 million. Not all the disasters were publicly traded stocks. There were scads of private companies like Miadora.com, the best online retail jewelry site. It raised $51 million in venture capital, burned through it, and closed down, all within 15 months.

Then there are the "winners" that still exist, with doors still open, whose stocks continue to trade albeit at a staggeringly discounted level. iVillage's zenith was $130, then aquired in single digits. Openwave Systems launched its IPO in mid-1999 at an equivalent of $48, shot up to $624 the following year at the height of the NASDAQ bubble, before its astounding collapse to $1. It's still alive but is now around $5. Wave Systems did its IPO at $15 in 1994, topping $143 in 2000, and then trading below $3 in 2006. It has reported nothing but red ink every quarter since becoming a publicly held company. VA Software (SourceForge) skyrocketed up to $239 from $30 after it became public in late 1999, and is now below $5. Yahoo!'s IPO was at $1.38 adjusted, it doubled its first day and ranged to over $120 before plunging into single figures. It has since recovered to about one-fifth of that high. Amazon.com, the champion, did its initial offering at $1.50 adjusted and saw its stock trade all the way to above $110, before tanking to below $6 prior to robust recovery. Japan's Internet-related wonder company, Softbank, has seen its shares dive a daunting 98.5%, from 198,000 yen to under 3,000 yen, according to *Economist* magazine. The granddaddy holding company that ruled the Internet universe, CMGI, the ultimate paradigm of the epoch, ascended to $163.50 before succumbing and being hammered to a low of $0.28. Countless '90s Bubble Era executives in the end created no value and drove their stocks to zero, yet a few lucky or cagey ones walked away with hundreds of millions or even a billion dollars.

Analysts were inundated with requests by institutions to track, even endorse these flashy new wave Internet entrants whose stocks were rocketing. Their ringmasters were youthful leaders who acted like Hollywood moguls, displaying massive overconfidence and off-putting attitudes. They were invited to investor conferences and their sessions were packed, given the mania for such risky high beta upstarts. The critical investment factors—real earnings, finances, and cash flow—were forgotten during that period. Such oversight is sometimes still evident today. The new stocks had absurdly high prices, tenuous business models, deficit prospects, and promotional management, so I viewed them as extremely risky speculations.

Historically, 8%–10% annual stock market returns have been the norm. In the late 1990s, the world turned upside down and market participants anticipated doubles, triples, and more as characterized by astounding, irrational stock price pinnacles. In the aftermath, while there has been some sobering atonement, investors still anticipate at least 10%–15% yearly gains. This presumption is not in line with past long-term results. Assume the market may appreciate 5%–10% over time, probably closer to 5% or less during the next few years.

Part and parcel of the absurd euphoria during that time was the annual November Comdex Conference in Las Vegas, by far the most outsized trade show in the country. At its peak in 2000, attendance reached 211,000. It was impossible to move around the strip, taxi lines snaked endlessly, stars like Bill Gates, Larry Ellison, Michael Dell, and John Chambers filled 5,000 seat theaters with at least that many being turned away. The number of corporate exhibitors crested at 2,337. What was once a personal computer forum had broadened to cover everything from consumer electronics to the Internet, computer services to semiconductors. There was free entertainment by rock bands and vocal celebrities. Along the way, Comdex (originally termed Computer Dealers Exposition) was sold for $860 million in 1995 to a Japanese entity. Guess that Japanese firm was caught up in the same ecstasy as Wall Street and its investors, bathed in rose-colored anticipation. The conference's demise was parallel to the bursting of the bubble. As a public company, it declared bankruptcy in 2003, and the entire Comdex trade show was cancelled in 2004. The end.

Research Runs Amuck

Research coverage and stock Buy ratings in the 1990s showed little differentiation between extremely speculative equities with red ink and little revenue, and established, stable, blue chip firms that had proven profit records. Analysts made no allowance for differing degrees of vulnerability among stocks they recommended. Investors were similarly indiscriminate. Companies with proven profits or precious assets should be valued accordingly. Investors must weigh the risks of firms whose outlook is vague. This element is paramount. The investor feeding frenzy in the 1990s demanded the most edgy, risky, newly public names. Those stock prices were ascending to unprecedented triple digit heights. Investors sought what was perceived as the best opportunity for the biggest gains from the most sexy, emerging, new wave companies. Analysts felt pressure from the sales force, trading, management, institutional clients, and retail investors to oblige. Long-standing, leading companies like General Electric, Citigroup, ExxonMobil, Wal-Mart, or Johnson & Johnson were boring. And there was little discretion with regard to market capitalizations—Yahoo!'s more than $100 billion value alone surpassing the entire auto industry. Pay careful attention to stock valuation and risk, integral to investing. They are still often disregarded by the Street.

Reports during the '90s Bubble Era became one-sided, all positive. No longer did the Street put negative concerns or risk factors into research commentary. Research now heard no feedback from compliance regarding the absence of any pessimistic topics in their reports. Stock recommendations altered into hype, promotion, and favorable prognostications. Lofty stock price targets helped tout the flattering story. When a price earnings ratio objective was not possible due to red ink far into the future, elevated price goals were justified by quantifying things like eyeballs viewing a website, clicks, market share, and revenue multiples.

The pathetic quality and blatant partiality of research done by analyst hype-artists of the time is elegantly portrayed by Roger Lowenstein of the *New York Times* in an article on the Adelphia scandal. His description of the research on the company during that era is revealing.

> "But what stands out from the analysts' reports is less the hype than the utter superficiality. Nowhere does a reader gain a feeling for what distinguished Adelphia – its cloistered weirdness, its familial obsessions, its precarious capital structure and persistent deficit of free cash flow. The analysts beat their breasts over minutiae, they obsess over stock charts, they deliver pages upon pages of spread sheets crammed with figures, yet nowhere do they scrutinize or even critically question the convenient company projections on which the numbers are based."

Research was further impacted by widespread arrogance during the 1990s bubble. This attitude of overconfidence exacerbated the eventual debacle. Analysts, portfolio managers, and investors couldn't imagine that at some point they might be wrong in their unrestrained enthusiasm. Their only fear was the possibility of missing out on the upside. Analysts lost touch with reality. There was no historical perspective, no balance, only a stridency in running with the bullish herd. Analysts seemed to be right out of central casting. They accentuated the pizzazz. It all went together—loss of objectivity, haughtiness, and indiscriminate promotion. A measure of the hubris has subsided but not totally dissipated. The exit of characters like Grubman and Blodget was a start, and sharply reduced analyst compensation has helped reestablish some humility. Curtailed or tightly controlled press contact has also contributed to a return of more modesty. But today there is still an abundant attitude of omniscience that exacerbates mistakes and wrong opinions.

Henry Blodget was perhaps the ultimate case of how attitude can be destructive. A youthful, collegiate, glib, precocious new arrival on Wall Street in 1994, he became an overnight sensation in late 1998, placing a $400 price target on Amazon.com, then trading at about $240. It zoomed above his outrageous goal within a month. An oracle of the New Economy, the press aggrandized him, and he basked in the limelight. He was the new breed of analyst, with no track record or seasoning. He had no MBA or CFA and was typical of the flock of novices that charged into the business in the 1990s. I called them bull market babies.

His Internet stocks propelled him into an über-analyst overnight. Blodget covered Internet Capital Group. It reached $212 before its steep plummet. His rating was still positive at $15, and today the stock is close to $10. His recommendation on 24/7 Real Media was favorable, while his internal email portrayed it as a "piece of s---," according to the legal evidence disclosed in all the press coverage. Its price swooned from over $60 to under $1. The news headline when he finally capitulated and reduced his opinions was "Now He Tells Us." In a settlement with the New York State Attorney General, Blodget is now banned forever from the securities industry.

Analyst hubris, celebrity, and overconfidence breeds mistakes. Fame can be intoxicating. The power to move stocks up or down sharply with a shift in a recommendation, all the corporate executive and media attention, and high poll rankings make analysts feel omnipotent. They start to believe that they are superior, puissant, and that's when the most egregious errors are committed. Distrust analysts appearing in the media too often. They are focused on pumping up their image as effulgent stars and not spending enough time doing research. Investors should put more credence in humble, unassuming analysts.

The security analyst profession should be like that of a neurosurgeon or heart specialist, where leading experts in the field are not household names. High TV visibility, and too much press, quotes, and media exposure tend to displace thoughtful, behind the scenes, quality research homework. It's more fun to be famous and blab to reporters and interviewers than to grind away in the office or in the field. And it's an ego trip. Brokerage firms should put extreme limits on analyst contact with media. This is starting to happen. There are fewer analyst talking heads these days, but it's still a compulsion. Analysts must act in a more professional manner, like CPAs and surgeons rather than sports figures and movie stars.

Events and Consequences of the Bubble Era Still Relevant

The bigger the party, the worse the hangover once reality resurfaces. Wall Street trust was broken in the 1990s aftermath. Even the New York Stock Exchange was sued. Mutual funds were discredited. Individual investors suffered massive wreckage. At home, day traders had to abandon their temporary retirement and again take on a real job. A friend of mine who's a therapist had to forgo retirement and again take on a full slate of patients. Given the market nose dive he had no trouble filling up his client list. As tax receipts plummeted and deficits amassed, governments faced the conundrum of markedly higher spending set during the boom and a reduction in proceeds in the more sober period that followed.

The crash, a term rarely used on the Street, led the exuberant, arrogant, and erroneous new wave analysts to their demise. In my view, some of them should have ended up in federal detention like Mike Milken in that sorry 1980s phase of pushing the junk bond envelope. But that didn't happen. The end of the abject display of superficial investment analysis—really just reporting, boosterism, and hawking— brought a lot of other Wall Street interests down to destruction with it.

A veil of tears was sewn in the profession during the bubble years, exposed in the subsequent collapse of the tech stocks and market.

The market was punctured and Bubble Era transgressions surfaced fast. Committees were established, procedures formalized, compliance oversight ballooned, brokerage management changed, rumors ran rampant, anxiety mounted. As revelations erupted, heads rolled. The market plunge halted banking deals and impacted commission revenues. Research budgets got whacked, partly from cost scrutiny, exacerbated by the loss of credibility and the absence of support from investment banking. Its cost was shifted from banking to sales, trading, and a more general corporate overhead. That led to even sharper examination of its merit. Management quickly assessed that an adequate product could be generated a lot cheaper by middle weight and junior analysts. Lay-offs ensued. Many of the more senior, highest paid analysts proved expendable in the new period of economic constraint.

Most analysts were not in the stock market business like I was during the 1970s bear market. Current analysts typically came along in the 1990s, maybe the late 1980s. They have no recollection of the three-year market swoon and subsequent years of doldrums during the 1970s. In the early 1970s it was conglomerates, one decision stocks, the Equity Funding fraud, and the Nifty Fifty. Growth stocks like Avon, Polaroid, Xerox, and Sony, expanding at a 15%-20% clip, sold at PE ratios in the 50x's. The first company I ever covered as a Wall Street analyst in 1971 was Automatic Data Processing (ADP). Since its growth rate was 25%-30% its PE was 100x. This was not considered abnormal, it was in line with other peers, so my initial rating was Buy. Extreme valuations proved in fact to be an aberration then and similarly absurd again in the 1990s. The stock market has become more rational since the latter bubble burst, but excesses during howling bull markets often take more than just a half dozen years to wring out.

Warren Buffet missed the incredible appreciation in Internet, tech, and telecom stocks during the late 1990s. Buffet is value oriented and only invests in companies he trusts and understands. A Luddite, he was mind boggled by the valuation absurdities. He had to excuse his performance at his annual meetings for a few years for missing the boat, not participating in the hysteria. Sticking to his guns, he became an idol again during the capitulation. Buffet couldn't bring himself to join in the irrationality of the era, believing a wrenching adjustment was forthcoming. You too have the freedom to avoid extremes and dodge the debacle that always follows. Institutional investors, most of whom must always be fully invested, do not have that luxury. Street analysts are similarly compelled to recommend stocks to feed insatiable institutional demand. You can stand aside during euphoric periods or when certain stock sectors get over heated. Extremes are unsustainable and always adjust precipitously.

Trustworthiness, sobriety, soundness. Investors must reflect these qualities. The extremes so evident in the '90s Bubble Era are relevant to your investment decisions today. But I am afraid that most investors have not yet adequately redressed the 1990s excesses. I fear that their memory is short, and the lessons have not been sufficiently learned. Investor expectations, stock valuations, and Street attitudes still display elements held over from that exultant period. Never forget the events and consequences of those years. They remain pertinent today.

The point of all this is that you need to grasp how Street analysts do research and how they have operated historically. Become your own analyst. Sometimes you can operate the same way. Conduct research like the insiders without the baggage, the biases, and the extraneous distractions. As an individual investor, you can investigate, listen to executives on conference calls, review earnings models, and act like a research analyst. Even those activities you are foreclosed from performing, like calling the CEO or attending a brokerage institutional investor conference, you can put in perspective by realizing how analysts orchestrate these research functions. It can pay to put yourself in the shoes of an analyst in certain instances, and at other times you can profit by going counter to their actions.

7

Reform Research to Level the Playing Field

A number of elements of Street research are detrimental to individual investors. There needs to be an array of alterations in the manner in which brokerage firms conduct research, to make the game more fair and to put individuals on par with professional Street insiders. The system that went so awry in the 1990s will not be corrected until all parties involved in the investment business have altered their behavior and are brought into the proper balance. Analysts hardly have time to conduct true research. They manage a team, grind out or massage intricate earnings models, tune in to incessant conference calls, attend meetings to deal with the bureaucracy, and scramble to respond to scores of telephone calls and emails from institutions, the sales force, and the press. Exigencies abound. On the road, they are booked solid with institutional client meetings all over town, with no time even for phone calls. Research is being relegated to a secondary support function and budgets slashed, with junior analysts proliferating as senior veterans depart. Analysis is being demoted, even outsourced, since it is of little benefit to the investment banking department or traders. Having lost credibility with individual investors, research has become a commoditized service for institutional investors like mutual funds.

Research Should Be More Autonomous

The misdeeds of analysts and their loss of objectivity are the fault of the system and a myriad of unrestrained influences. That is what needs reform. A whole new research model is required. There should be more separation, not just from investment banking as is already the case, but also from the sales force, corporate executives, and institutional investors. Although analysts can no longer be paid directly for or involved in bringing in or executing investment banking business, guess what? Duh...research opinions are still skewed in favor of investment banking clients.

Analysts confront an assortment of influences; it's impossible to serve all the groups effectively. It's an absurd balancing act. The brokerage firm trader on the desk gets the first call from the analyst, as traders scramble to make a few cents per share on a stock trade in an hour or two. The institutional sales force covering the portfolio managers at places like SAC Capital, Putnam Management, or T. Rowe Price want the analyst's insight to generate a commission-producing transaction that day, with maybe a month or two time horizon for the idea to work. The director of research emphasizes analyst poll rankings in order to look good with upper management. The analyst is totally aware of all investment banking relationships the firm has with the companies he covers, another factor subtly weighing on the research. Retail brokers (sometimes termed financial consultants or account executives) dealing with individual investors need objective research and effective stock picking. Brokerage firms should step back and reconfigure all research to properly address each constituency.

Street research needs more autonomy from all bodies attempting to influence analyst thinking. Analysts should be shielded from being bulldozed by buyside clients and in-house salespeople, traders, bankers, and management. They should be akin to auditors, judges, and sports officials. Their role as impartial advisers must be restored. We need built-in safeguards to enable unbiased views and to prevent recourse if recommendations are unpopular. At present, analysts are overly hesitant to adopt pessimistic opinions, fearing backlash from all the research constituencies and corporate executives.

Analysts generate commission dollars for the firm. Institutions allocate stock trades and orders to a brokerage firm in return for valuable input or research help from the analyst. Research is a value-added service being rendered to the client, but buyside payment to brokerages for this service does not go directly to the research department. Transactions go to the institutional and private client salespeople. They get credit for the revenue. The research budget is defrayed by sales. And research leaders then bow to sales force demands. These are just the conflicts originating from within the analyst's own firm.

Analysts are susceptible to the demands of the institutional sales force, the source of a major portion of the research budget, whose motive is usually to generate immediate trades. Institutional and retail clients represent two disparate research audiences, each having distinct requirements. Research is pulled in dissimilar directions. The brokerage institutional sales force conducts an annual analyst evaluation, an important measurement in compensation. It's a conflict, because analysts strive for good marks by appealing in a popularity poll with short-term trading focused ideas rather than providing considered, longer term, investment oriented research. In attempting to please all research users, the product is twisted in so many directions it is ill-suited to any one of the audiences.

Outside of the firm, institutional clients want industry and company insight, forecasts, trends, analysis, interpretation, and views. Major buyside institutions' in-house security analysts consume hours of brokerage analysts' time, obtaining a more thorough understanding of companies. These insiders are mildly interested in our stock recommendations, but they treat them lightly. Hedge funds are almost the opposite, and are always angling to shape analysts' opinions in line with their short or long positions. There are too many disproportionate forces compelling analysts to cater heavily to major institutional investment clients, like hedge funds, that generate the bulk of commission revenues to brokerage firms.

A new model to pay for research will be necessary in the future. The investment banking function is now detached from research and no longer renders financial support. Commission rates are diminishing, dropping 18% annually in the U.S. in recent years; the price for an institutional trade is now only a few pennies per share. Fidelity is pushing to unbundle commission rates, for a rock-bottom "execution only" price tag, in order to forgo paying for research it doesn't want. Electronic institutional trading commissions are less than a penny per share. Because hedge funds trade so actively, their total commission generation is inordinately heavy, giving their hot money undue sway over research analysts. The hedgies and big gorilla institutions demand special treatment from analysts. They expect insights, nuances, and observations, almost like a consulting arrangement. The rest of the clients and investors make do with a written report or commentary on a mass conference call.

Commission revenue allocated to research has been cut in half over the last five years, according to Greenwich Associates. The Street is reducing research budgets, outsourcing, and downsizing analyst staffs. Morgan Stanley announced such a curtailment in 2006, and Goldman Sachs before that. Research has become a backwater. Prudential Financial closed down its stock research department altogether in mid-2007, laying off about 420 people. Institutional investors have been spoiled by receiving all brokerage services, including research, on a bundled basis. They will not pay for such services separately, having become accustomed to getting all research for free; that is, in return for their commission payments. So, brokers are shifting toward adding junior-level analysts at modest pay levels, bodies to cover the waterfront in terms of stocks. Research is becoming a mile wide and an inch deep. Investment banking indirectly may again play a role in justifying research. The goal seems to be to cover numerous names with less-seasoned analysts, just in case there might be some banking business that comes along. Obviously, a firm is not in the running for an investment banking deal unless there is research coverage, despite the cleanup since the 1990s bubble misdeeds. The way things are heading, and regardless of attempts to uncouple banking from research, it appears that conflicts will remain in the future.

Research should be spun off as a separate arms-length entity. Brokerage firms should detach this function just like their investment management and mutual fund units. Analysts need more separation from the sales force and traders (the break away from investment banking is already evident), and from the executives of the companies they cover. The Elliot Spitzer-required independent research provided by several Street firms has not been the answer. Many of these entities offer the same three or four pages of data on a stock, slap on their own cover page opinion and conclusion, and push that out as research. It's basically just boilerplate.

Research departments should charge hard dollar fees just like any consultant or other professional service. This would aid objectivity and enhance quality since poor research would not attract paying clients. A shakeout would occur, with more pure competition as the result. No longer would analysts be ranked according to popularity and intensity of communications. Research must add value to gain fee-generating institutional customers. Such payments for research should also be required of the institutional sales desk and retail brokers of the parent brokerage firm. Many brokerages might eliminate research and use the research entities of others, which would result in more independence.

Alter Compensation and Make Research Less Expensive

Wall Street has always been massively overcompensated. Its denizens earn several multiples of what counterparts might gross in another industry. That includes doctors, attorneys, and corporate executives like CFOs. The only comparison might be sports figures, entertainers, and certain CEOs. An analyst's preparation, education, training, and professional qualifications are minimal compared to these other vocations. Relatively junior analysts get paid $150,000–$500,000. Senior analysts who have been in the business a decade or so, and are *I.I.* ranked, can still clear $1 million annually, although that is down from $2–$6 million during the '90s Bubble Era. This gives analysts an overblown sense of importance. It can lead to arrogance and a certain hubris.

Research must become less expensive. The mindset in the past was to maintain a stable of all-stars who rack up votes in the *Institutional Investor* poll rankings. So, the tendency over the years has been to hire ranked analyst teams at excessive prices, and lock them in for two or three years under a guaranteed contract with no commensurate performance requirements. Firms are vulnerable to the mercenary jumping ship after the contract is finished. The analyst is under no commitment to achieve milestones. No bonus incentive is dependent on attaining any pre-established goals. All the analyst has to do is stay employed. Sharply higher compensation attracts prominent analysts to come on board. It is like a free agent in professional sports. But embarrassing disparities develop with the comp level of similarly distinguished analysts already at a firm for several years. Analysts who remain with a firm for a decade or two sometimes are not paid at a level commensurate with a new hotshot hired from another firm. Something is wrong with this system. Contracts were curtailed during the 2001–2002 contraction but are resurfacing again these days. There needs to be a greater premium on analyst longevity.

Analyst compensation is not based on accuracy of investment opinions, earnings estimate precision, or other calculable measures. Unlike the brokerage sales force that can be judged on the commission dollars it generates, the research analyst's performance is judged more qualitatively. It's almost a popularity contest. One of the more precise, scientific outside assessments of analysts is the Greenwich Survey, but because it's low profile, it has only minor weight. One key ingredient of analyst remuneration is effectiveness with major institutional clients. This translates into grants of commission business. The institution commits to do a certain amount of commissions, say $10,000, with a brokerage firm each quarter to pay for the help from a particular analyst. And there are also sales force and institutional investor surveys and flawed peer group cross evaluations. But analyst pay is still largely a judgment call. Revamping compensation and tying it directly to the correctness of analysts' advice would be a giant leap toward emphasizing the proper priority and ensuring objectivity. Analysts would never permit other influences to color their views if their compensation depended on their opinion accuracy. It would be the ultimate truth serum.

Investment research is presumably the key to determining which stocks should outperform and which should underperform over the long-term, defined as at least a one- or two-year span. If the charter is for *investment* research, then the measurement needs to be on a one- to two-year time frame. If that's the goal, then the bulk of an analyst's compensation should be based directly on the precision of these calls. Accurate Sell recommendations should be valued just as highly as correct Buy opinions. Firms that utilize research to produce short-term trading ideas will judge analyst calls perhaps on a quarterly basis, which is an entirely different type of security analysis. Even the pay of mutual fund portfolio managers is misaligned, being heavily based on assets under management. What a surprise to see Janus's new chief investment officer a couple years ago overhaul its reward structure, keying it more to "competitive performance, first and foremost."

As Wall Street commissions shrink and research budgets are trimmed, the old method of maintaining an assortment of stars has degenerated, putting research into disarray. When an established analyst departs, it's a stretch to afford a similar replacement. There's still a desire to rank high on the *I.I.* poll, to hire such leading analysts, but the means to pay for these heavyweights are gone. A number of these eminent analysts are walking away from the Street. As a result, a steadily rising premium is being placed on cultivating new talent internally. Although a few firms like Goldman Sachs are effective with this formula, most brokers are of the old school and are now suffering the consequences. Efforts to hire carefully and to develop junior analysts are often frustrating. As junior analysts mature and take on more responsibility, research management is hard-pressed to recognize their progress and reward them with appropriate incentives. The economics of developing minor leaguers inside a firm so they later reach the major league level are compelling but necessitate a long-term view, foreign to most research directors.

Fewer Distractions and More Time for Research Needed

As a seasoned analyst, I was probably typical, spending about 20% of my time actually conducting research activities. *Institutional Investor* magazine published an article several years ago on the "Secrets of the Superstars." It listed analyst work priorities by importance, and the key Wall Street research analyst focus had nothing to do with research or recommendations—it was communications with clients. This priority indicates the upside-down emphasis of marketing over research analysis. Following that main thrust were other critical preoccupations: staying in companies' good graces, juggling investment banking demands, providing global coverage, working with junior analysts, and lastly...finding time for research!

Institutions make constant demands on analysts, insist they bring management of the companies under coverage to their cities for meetings, require exclusive one-on-one executive meetings at conferences, and press analysts to call them first with insightful tidbits and nuances. Their every whim is made a priority. Analysts are sucked into this vortex. We are called securities analysts, but a more apt moniker is research communicators. Analysts spend double or triple the time on investor/client contact compared to research analysis. It is far more important. Research and work hours are lopsided.

Analysts chew up most of their day talking to key clients and the sales desk, and in other marketing activities like traveling to meet with institutional investors or making road show forays with managements. Travel is incessant. While based on the west coast, I made 18 trips to the east coast one year, my personal best. Often analysts head out on Sundays and don't get back until Friday night. Weekends are frequently disrupted by business trips. In the office, we scramble all day, reacting to stock price moves, rumors, press releases, accusations, and news. We constantly get inquiries from institutional analysts and portfolio managers, the institutional and retail sales forces, traders, the press, and others. We spend time in discussion with the other analysts and support staff in our groups. Handheld Blackberry email devices, cell phones, and laptops go with us everywhere. I don't bother shutting down these electronics as requested on airplane flights, because sometimes there's reception at 30,000 feet.

At some point, the Street started to put speed ahead of everything else. And institutional investors began to demand an instant take in almost every situation. So, analysts now must act and deliver their thoughts hurriedly. Speed is as important as accuracy, which I view as a flawed priority. No reaction or a delayed one is not an option. We are required to have an instant evaluation of surprising and confusing events. Facts are always incomplete. Prior to flushing out details with executives, the analyst must gauge whether the matter has a material influence on earnings forecasts or the near-term health of the company. Equally important is our impression of the impact it might have on the stock price. Time is critical. We are compelled to jump on the firm-wide speaker box system and give our views within minutes. It's okay not to have specifics on revised estimates or the magnitude of effect on the company, but we must communicate a sense of overall importance, direction, and influence on future prospects. And our demeanor under fire needs to be insouciant, measured, and confident in order to impart an air of credibility.

Street research analysts are under a constant barrage of pressure, always reacting, scrambling, and on the move. Their travel, 24-hour on call communications, instant analysis, and speed—and the trading mentality of their major constituents—leave precious little time to conduct quality, thoughtful research.

Former Analysts Ill-Equipped to Manage Research

A big problem with research is that it is customarily supervised by former analysts. Sector leaders are almost always analysts and have minimal background in how to be effective heads of a unit. They frequently lack the proficiency to encourage, empower, support, direct, mentor, or inspire. The ex-inmates are running the asylum. And just try to organize a flock of arrogant, highly-paid rock stars. And yes, they know research all right, but they don't have a clue how to be effective leaders of a department. Analysts are like consultants or professional golfers; basically loners, never having had any experience in playing on a team or directing an organization. More professional leadership with farsighted vision is needed. Powerful, established, competent analysts cannot be managed. They need to be empowered. Instead, these days they are being constrained with heavy oversight. It's another reason why I and countless other senior analysts have exited the business.

Until the bubble burst, there was a less burdensome management structure. Established analysts had freer reign. That was before research mushroomed into an uncontrollable morass. Once the markets tanked and legal issues came to the forefront, the stage was set. Weighty management muscled up—as if on steroids—despite analyst layoffs. A decade ago, about the only internal analyst reporting tasks were annual reviews of staff and cross-evaluations amongst peers. Added to that now are requirements like annual business plans, mid-year plan reviews, mid-year staff reviews, twice-a-year investment committee assessment, opinion change committee sessions, recommended list oversight group meetings, mandatory legal compliance briefings, organized training classes, departmental meetings, monthly group leader sessions—you get the idea. I estimate that all the internal requirements from management now take at least 10%–15% of analysts' time compared to less than 1% in pre-bureaucratic times.

Research management is cautious by nature, and these days it is hogtied with bureaucratic legal compliance. There is a labyrinth of committees and approval processes. Meetings and directives abound. Leaders are protecting their backsides from being dragged into more lawsuits. These new regulatory and legal guidelines are a thicket. All this supersedes the real analyst job of producing quality, forthright, useful, timely research.

Research should be directed by a single voice. The excess layers of management are dumbfounding. Before the 1990s rush, most firms had one director of research. There was one sole decision maker, and it was clear who took care of research issues. The management style was hands-off. It wasn't possible for one person to over-manage dozens of analysts. And it worked well, before the hoard of unqualified, out of control analysts beholden to investment banking flooded into research during the frothy 1990s bull market. Now it is the opposite extreme. It is common to have several research managers at the same time. Multiple managers mean no one makes a decision. Analysts often don't know whom to contact on any given issue. Most managers avoid making definitive decisions. The right hand frequently fails to talk to the left hand. The rules keep changing for analysts. Policies at brokerage firms shift constantly, almost arbitrarily, and it's inconsistent. The hoops they must jump through dilute the time for research. There ought to be clearer delineations of authority. Analysts are hamstrung by having to cater to the sensitivities of the multi-layered organization.

Management turnover also diminishes analyst productivity. More management consistency and a simpler overhead structure would help. Analysts often need to start over from scratch and brainwash the new leaders, painstakingly briefing them, readjusting to trifling new procedures, telling them what they want to hear. Management new to the scene does not remember what was promised or decided the year before, regarding things such as compensation, staff, conferences, and other plans. The approval and justification process is repeated again from scratch. It's frustrating.

Investment committees are another dysfunctional aspect of Street research. These disparate management groups review opinion ratings and potential changes with analysts, sitting in front of stock charts armed with only snippets of understanding and information on any particular company. They are influenced by recent stock price actions, and being highly reactionary, are quick to pull the trigger, with little long-term investment horizon. Such clumsy group over-sight is an impediment to crisp decisions and steady, consistent investment recommendations.

Analysts cannot serve two masters. Securities research should be structured similarly to retail merchandizing—that is, wholesale to institutions, retail to individuals. This may require separate research departments and different analysts. Of course, the push has been to equalize the research product for all audiences, so regulators might take issue with separate treatment, figuring that the retail individual investor would be a stepchild. But the needs are vastly different. Individual research should be thematic, with long-range investment objectives, clearly indicating degree of risk, always assuming the user is a naive, uninformed consumer. This audience should not be misled with stock price objectives. Notable, bold print warnings similar to a cigarette package should be glaringly evident in these reports, alerting small investors to the fallibility and variability of the research recommendations.

Require More Research Accountability

Professional credentials should be required of analysts. Every other profession has serious mandatory qualifications: accountants—CPAs, attorneys—bar exams, medical doctors—state boards, architects, engineers all have exams, licenses, and strict requirements. There are no such prerequisites to be a Street securities analyst. Incredibly, the CFA is voluntary. Even an MBA degree is optional. Back in 1971, I needed an MBA just to get interviews on the Street. Such standards should be the norm now. All new analysts should pass level 1 of the CFA before being given authority to establish stock opinions and recommendations. That initial level must be compulsory for all analysts within, say, 3 years of their entry in the business. And the level 3 full CFA title needs to be obligatory for all senior analysts. The security analyst position ought to be a more formal profession.

Research analysts should assume fiduciary responsibility. Because analysts render authoritative advice that has major financial implications, there should be a more formal, legal trustworthiness behind their actions as there is for investment managers. It is my opinion that they need to be subject to malpractice suits for misconduct. Legal responsibility should pertain to professional conduct, not to accuracy of findings. The French company Moët Hennessy Louis Vuitton sued Morgan Stanley over errors in research that unjustly denigrated it. This is a conundrum, as analysts need to feel free to make critical judgements, but they must also be held accountable to professional standards.

The first baby step in higher accountability was the addition in research reports of a statement certifying that the analyst's written opinion was truly his own personal view. But it's not enough. Like medical doctors, attorneys, and CPAs, analysts must have a fiduciary obligation to conduct their business in a *professional* manner. Why are investment managers held liable for their conduct and not security analysts, who can have far broader impact on corporations, investors, and stocks? A more precisely defined duty to operate in a responsible, qualified, professional fashion would add more gravity to Street actions and is sorely needed in the aftermath of the 1990s bubble market absurdities.

Analysts must be protected from conflicting interests of brokerage management. There are glaring conflicts of interest with research at the upper management levels of most brokerage firms. Instances where the CEO or other top executives of a firm have reached down to analysts to influence coverage, investment ratings, and the tone of commentary are widespread. Perhaps the most notorious case was at Citigroup, when Sandy Weill urged Jack Grubman, at Citi's wholly owned Salomon Smith Barney entity, to take a "fresh look" at AT&T just before that firm chose its bankers for a lucrative underwriting deal. Any communications from brokerage management to analysts must be treated similarly to investment banking contact—that is, to be done in the presence of legal compliance. This would curtail coercion to participate in questionable deals, to visit companies and executives that the analyst is hesitant about, and to do research conflicting with the best interests of investors.

Brokerage executives should be barred from corporate boards of directors. This is a massive conflict of interest, raising potential inside information issues. Goldman Sachs no longer permits its executives to serve on outside boards. At the very least, research coverage should be prohibited on any company where an executive from the brokerage firm serves on the board. The situation when an analyst has a favorable opinion, and one of his firm's executives sits on that company's board, just plain looks bad, straining credibility. The integrity of research cannot tolerate this type of dissonance.

Research must be disconnected from corporate investment banker selection. A paragraph should be required in every deal prospectus certifying that executives chose the investment banking firm based on considerations that completely exclude research factors. The analyst's coverage and investment rating during the period the company was appraising and making its banker selection should be stated in that paragraph. This disclosure would make any incestuous, cozy, preferential, and biased analyst relationship with company management more obvious to investors. The clause should also detail the analyst's communications and involvement with the corporate executives regarding the investment banking association and any direct contact regarding the deal. Security analysts are not isolated enough from the corporate clients of the investment banks at which they work. If they cover a company that completes a stock offering or major merger or acquisition deal, research is only suspended temporarily. The restricted period is just 40 days following an offering. There is an understood expectation by a company's executives that the analyst will reinstate coverage after this limited time span with a positive opinion. The restriction time should be 6 months or even a year, to amply disconnect research coverage from an investment banking transaction. That would discourage corporate executives from expecting enthusiastic support from the analyst as part and parcel of the investment banking relationship.

Institutional Investors Should Play by the Same Rules

Reforms are necessary not only to sellside brokerage firm research but also to buyside institutions. Certain actions of the mutual funds, investment managers, insurance companies, banks, pension funds, and hedge funds are detrimental to the individual investor. It's not fair. Reforms of the buyside institutional investors are critical to balance out the system. Hedge funds are the single element of Wall Street that continues out of control with no alteration in behavior since the excesses of the '90s Bubble Era. The Spitzer-induced modifications to brokerage firm and mutual fund practices have not branched out to the unregulated Wild West ways of hedgehogs. And this money is not merely wealthy individuals making speculative investments. Massive state pension funds and corporate retirement assets are being poured into these risky, unfettered investment pools that need not play the game by the standards established for the rest of the market.

You'd be amazed at the advantage mega-institutional holders have in gaining access to corporate management when sitting with a multi-million share position. Buyside meetings with executives at headquarters should be open to other attendees, buy and sell side, or at least be webcast to all comers. One-on-one confabs with management at analysts' conferences should also be more open and more equal. For at least 48 hours after they conclude a meeting or a full-blown conference call with any corporation's executives, buyside investors should be prohibited from conducting transactions involving the stock of that enterprise. The inordinate influence that big holders have over executives must be restricted. Buyside access to exclusive information must be curtailed.

Unsavory tactics need to be forbidden; such as an institution verbally promoting a stock that it currently is selling, or comments by an institution to drive a stock lower in order to purchase it cheaper. Sellside analysts must not hold or communicate opinions contrary to their published recommendation. The buyside must also be held to such behavior standards. Self-serving commentary to boost the price of an existing holding should be banned. Hedge funds should be barred from bad-mouthing companies in which they hold short positions; and the same principle should apply to *all* overt acts that may affect stock prices for self-serving reasons.

Broader disclosure should be required by major stockholders. Currently, only shareholders owning more than 5% of a company's stock must report their position in an SEC filing. Corporations disclose these biggest holders in their annual proxy statements. Typically, there are only one or two large holders, if any, so there is a shroud of mystery regarding, say, holders owning 1% to 5% who might also have undue access to or influence on executives. Any owner of more than 1% or maybe 2% of a stock should be revealed by corporations and holders in their filings, and it should be quarterly. This would expose potential sources of power that might use their sway to extract information from or excessively pressure executives. More detailed reporting of major stockholders in a company will reduce the tendency of executives to play favorites with select buyside institutions.

Institutional holdings and changes should be reported more often. Currently, mutual funds reveal their lineup of stocks quarterly. Hedge funds are not required to ever publish their positions. The cloak over institutional portfolios leaves room for devious maneuvers and manipulative shenanigans at the end of each quarter. Sellside analysts' opinion changes are disseminated widely on an immediate basis. In the interest of greater transparency, institutional investors should be required to report their trades within days of each transaction. More instant daylight will discourage a lot of connivery.

Buyside professionals should be prohibited from personally owning stocks held by their funds. There are too many potential conflicts of interest here. Institutional portfolio managers cannot be allowed to personally own any stocks that are held in the funds they manage. Buyside analysts should be prohibited from investing in any stocks they cover, just like the sellside. They need to be held to the same standards as sellside analysts.

The compensation of portfolio managers and senior analysts should be disclosed. Top corporate executives' remuneration is reported annually in proxy statements. It is subject to the review of shareholders. The same should hold true for all institutional portfolio managers and senior analysts at brokerage firms and institutions. It would encourage more restraint and gravity. The constituencies, such as mutual fund holders and sellside research users, would have more influence if there were more scrutiny. Absurd compensation levels would generate skepticism, and require justification. And sunshine

might bring moderation, even sanity, to the business. It just seems
healthier to have fuller disclosure here.

Corporate Executives Are Part of the Problem

Investment research reforms must also extend to public corporations
and executives. There has been a transformation in publicly-held
companies from traditional owners' capitalism to the current era of
managers' capitalism. Executives now operate as if they own the company rather than being hired hands, which is their proper role. Excessive compensation, stock options, overboard perks, and absurd
actions to boost immediate profitability all come at the expense of
long-term public shareholder interests. Although founders who still
own sizeable stock positions in their public company should be
allowed some leeway, too many CEOs act like they started up the
business. The problem this presents for securities analysts and
investors is that executives treat them as pawns, to serve their own
personal financial interests. Executive behavior with Wall Street is
warped toward manipulating the stock price; biased embellishment
of upbeat news and favorable factors, nondisclosure or underempha-
sis of gloomy aspects. Company managements must be constrained
from self-serving practices to subjectively persuade analysts and
investors of the stock potential. There exists a systemic conflict of interest between executives and analysts.

Deficiencies in Wall Street research have a more pronounced impact
on individual investors than on professional institutional insiders. New
approaches are necessary by research management at brokerage firms.
Buyside institutions (such as mutual funds and hedge funds), the SEC,
and publicly-held companies must also change their ways. But so far,
the attitude of all these parties toward the individual investor has been
phlegmatic. Reforms such as separation of research and analyst compensation based on opinion accuracy could vastly improve the current
discredited state of research. But to achieve such a revamp, an entire
new research model may be required. The Street needs to approach
research more creatively and more professionally. Until that happens,
individual investors will just have to work around the Street, exploit it,
and in the end be their own securities analysts.

Afterword

Overhaul your approach to investing. Invest the right way. Revamp your practices. Realign your investing strategies. By digesting the observations and exhortations in this book, conscientious investors will be able to understand how Wall Street really operates, how it plays the game, and how they can improve their investment performance. Separate babble from substance, regardless of whether the source of that blather is Wall Street, the media, or companies. Don't rely on the Street. Warren Buffet's attitude is, "Never ask the barber if you need a haircut." When you ask a brokerage which stock to buy, the firm invariably advocates what it wants to sell, not what might be the best investment for you.

What do you think a brokerage opinion of Hold/Aggressive indicates? The term is meaningless. Yet this type of jargon is what we get from the Street. You should use the Street the same way you would employ *The Wall Street Journal*, a friend's investment suggestion, or any investment idea that comes to mind. That is, view the Street as just one among many sources of information pertaining to potential investment strategies and opportunities. Like any input, the information it offers is only a starting point—not a final conclusion. Don't take Wall Street literally. Put it in the proper perspective. Do what Wall Street does, not what it says. *Use its information and its research content, not its conclusions or recommendations.* Remember, most professional portfolio managers who run mutual funds have mediocre investment performance records. Street analyst opinions are even worse; analysts can't pick stocks. There's a famous assessment of securities analysts by Gerald Loeb: "In a bull market, you don't need them. In a bear market, you don't want them." Research reports are never complete, forthright, balanced, or objective. They are good for background, but are not actionable. Be vigilant of all the Street's shortcomings, which exceed even those of the media and of corporate executives (and their typically optimistic predilection). Corporate management should be utilized in the same manner as Street analysts—to gain an understanding about a company and industry trends, not for investment guidance.

I am often asked about my daily investment regimen. Since I no longer have to work at the office from 6 to 5, I tune into CNBC and Bloomberg Television every morning with my first cup of coffee and (after poring over the sports page) study *The New York Times* business section and *The Wall Street Journal*. Then I ensconce myself at my computer to peruse my holdings and any pertinent company or industry sector news. On the weekends, I look through *The Economist* and I cannot live without *Barron's*. Online, I access relevant articles in *Forbes*, *BusinessWeek*, and other investment or business magazines. I tap into conference call replays in my car if I have a drive of at least 45 minutes. And on an Excel spreadsheet, I track key data on my stocks: date of purchase, original price, estimated dividends, yield, and gains and losses. Because my brokerage accounts are online, I can monitor them regularly. All this activity is day-to-day and week-to-week, but my best thinking occurs while secluded on an airplane or at a vacation resort, pondering, strategizing, and forming views on the bigger long-term picture.

Invest for the Long Haul; Be Patient and Realistic

Since retiring from the Wall Street cauldron, I have become an individual investor, free from the constraints that entangle most insiders and the systemic influences that bias the Street. I make time to read the financial press, assess the markets and my stocks online, chat with investor friends, and periodically review my investment strategy and portfolio. I always try to be open to tweaking my investment positions, but vigilant in guarding against the urge to make a trade based on a short-term catalyst. Invariably, doing nothing has proven to be a sounder long-term approach than making a lot of shifts in my holdings. As an individual investor, you, too, are free to do the right thing. But that freedom also enables you to make foolish mistakes that professionals tend to avoid.

I've been away from the Wall Street circus for five years now. That distance gives me a perspective that combines an insider's knowledge with an outsider's objectivity. Having read this book, you also possess the same advantage—not only an awareness of the strange Street practices but the ability to make your own detached investment decisions. I find that my investing has improved since I exited Wall Street. I can take a more distant view and have time to devote to my portfolio. While I was a security analyst, my investments were almost entirely in the computer services stocks that I covered. My delicate position precluded active buying and selling, and I was required to hold the stocks for many years. Fortunately, the computer services business was exceptionally stable and consistent, while expanding at a healthy clip. The industry was an ideal growth stock sector at that time. The long-term nature of my holdings necessitated patience in my personal investment practice. This trait has become even more pronounced now that I'm no longer exposed to all the Wall Street noise and distractions. A longer time horizon is essential to proper investing.

Perseverance must be accompanied by realistic performance goals. Aim for 5%–10% annual total return including dividends, 15% would be spectacular. Be patient, long-term oriented, and have reasonable expectations. In the mid-1980s, EDS, a stock I covered intensely, was merging with General Motors. One member of management, a Texan who was one of EDS's first employees and played an integral on-scene role as a part of the company's harrowing Iran hostage rescue, decided to opt out and start up his own oil-drilling company. He hung up his business suit and started wearing blue jeans to his modest office. What surprised me, when I inquired about his new venture, was his limited objective of achieving a mere 10%–15% annual return. I was from Wall Street and therefore accustomed to 20%–30% growth stock targets. His business plan was to buy up small, remote wells, maintain a low-cost overhead, and attain profitability even if the price of oil was just $5–$10 a barrel. The price of oil moved from the teens to $20, and after a few years, he and his handful of private investors began to generate some robust returns. But the ongoing aim remained a 10%–15% return. The oil price was below $20 for much of the 1990s but, given its low cost-structure, that was not a problem for the new company. Now, more than 20 years later, with the price of oil per barrel climbing above $70, just imagine the gains!

Once I dropped off the Wall Street payroll, my investment strategy shifted to an emphasis on consistent, reliable, income-producing securities. My priority became protection of capital and income generation, not capital gains. The first major position in my portfolio was an oil pipeline and storage royalty trust that was listed on the NYSE and carried a dividend yield of around 7%. The business was consistent and predictable. Oil flows through the pipelines and is stored in tanks, creating ongoing revenue regardless of oil price fluctuations. All I wanted was to take home my 7% dividend and keep risk to a minimum. A humble attitude is a characteristic that is as important for investors as it is for corporate executives. And *voilà*, over the ensuing four years, I watched with delight as the dividend was boosted by almost 50% and the share price doubled. This fabulous performance was just icing on the cake.

If you are at my stage in life, living on a more fixed income, you face the investment question of growth versus income. High-yield value investments should constitute the bulk of a senior person's portfolio; no more than 20%, maybe even as little as 10%, of such a portfolio should be devoted to growth stocks. This stance is geared toward protecting capital. Growth stocks are risky and volatile. They might be thrilling if you need excitement, but the rush will quickly vanish after their decimation in the next bear market. I don't buy the thesis that growth stocks are necessary to keep pace with the overall market and economy. Low PE-multiple income stocks perform just fine in a rising market. Any growth-oriented equities should be held in an Individual Retirement Account (IRA) or other tax-advantaged account. I live off the income generated from my portfolio, so I avoid locking up dividend income in my retirement accounts.

Dividend and interest income should be derived from both bonds and stocks, with at least half attained from the former. I feel strongly about shielding capital, especially at this point in life. Obtain higher yield with income stocks, royalty trusts, REITs, or even preferred stocks (however, as noted earlier, I recommend that your stocks in all of these categories be NYSE-listed). Income stocks may generate dividend yields above 5%, sometimes close to 10%. But be careful.

Heightened risk accompanies yields in the 10% range. There's no free lunch. A few years ago, I coasted along with Calpine (a California utility) bonds that were paying more than 10%. My assumption was that electrical utility firms never go bankrupt. What a surprise when I discovered that this one did! My losses far exceeded all the interest I'd earned in the prior years. The conservative avenue to maximizing income is to seek quality stocks yielding around 5% that have good prospects for raising their dividends in the future. That way, based on the original purchase price, there is the potential to obtain a 10% yield down the road.

Exploit Your Status as an Individual Investor

Conduct your own research. Observe. Read. Listen. Overhear. Ponder. Anticipate. Predict. Analyze. Question. Judge. Be skeptical. When evaluating companies as potential investments, seek out specialty firms—they do it better than generalists. The business should be relatively simple to understand. Financial strength is paramount. Assess the value of its assets. The five- or ten-year earnings record is important. But nothing is perfect. Some variation in earnings performance is natural and inevitable. Assessing corporate management requires scrutinizing quality, character, values, and attitude. An important trait in a company's executives is humility. Steer clear of arrogant executives. Be wary of spin and self-promotion. Ray DeVoe, the market observer, contends "Good judgment comes from experience, and experience comes from bad judgment. But bad judgment is just a polite term for stupidity." I hope this book helps you avoid the latter.

Finally, apply the soundest investment strategies. Be patient. Invest long-term; don't trade. Look for value. Seek dividends. Don't spread yourself too thin; limit the number of stocks you own so that you can pay proper attention to each one. Keep it simple; nothing too exotic. **Preserve your capital.** If you can manage to avoid shrinkage in your overall portfolio, performance will take care of itself, and you will achieve excellent long-term results. It's not what you make, it's what you keep. Investment risk (the possibility of permanent loss of capital) and price valuation are critical factors when looking at a stock, but they are usually overlooked in the pursuit of big gains from "new era" investment ideas. Consistency is more important than absolute appreciation. Don't be fooled by the Street. You're no longer an amateur playing against professionals. Invest intelligently, take advantage of the Street, and outflank the experts to make money in the market.

Glossary

'90s Bubble Era The years during late 1990s ending with the March 2000 stock market decline when euphoria reigned, especially in high-tech, Internet, telecom, and a few other stock sectors. Investment bank brokerage firms went wild with initial public offerings (IPOs). Analysts lost all sense of objectivity in promoting speculative, excessively priced stocks.

10-K report An annual filing to the SEC required of publicly held companies that includes extensive financials and commentary on the business. Widely available to the public.

10-Q report A quarterly filing to the SEC required of publicly held companies, less detailed than the 10-K, includes financials and commentary on the business. Widely available to the public.

Accounts receivable turnover The average time period a company is owed funds from its customers for sales transactions. Granting of credit extends the time of collection. Ninety days is a standard. The time is calculated by dividing annualized revenues by average accounts receivable, and dividing that into 365 days.

ADR (American Depository Receipt) A certificate in the holder's name indicating ownership of a non-U.S. company's stock; the actual shares of the foreign company are held at a U.S. bank's foreign branch.

Annual report A publication by a publicly held company discussing the year's results, including extensive financials (sometimes contains the 10-K report) and often reviewing the company's business and outlook.

Axe (in a stock) A Street analyst with the reputation for doing the best research and being the most knowledgeable on a given stock.

Balance sheet A financial statement that includes assets (such as cash and accounts receivable) on one side, and liabilities (such as debt) and stockholders equity on the other.

Bear market   A material, enduring decline in stock prices of at least 20% over a period of more than one year. Broad-based investor pessimism and negative sentiment. Ten bear markets have occurred since 1946 according to S&P, with the average drop of more than 30% during a span of 16 months. On average, it required 22 months to recover all the way back. The most notable bear markets were the 1930s and 1967–1993 periods.

Big/large cap stock   A company with total shares outstanding having a value or capitalization of at least $5–$10 billion in the stock market.

Black Swan event   A highly improbable event that has an extreme impact, readily explainable after the fact, but always a surprise, as defined in the book *Black Swan* by Nassim Taleb.

Blackberry   A portable, handheld email, phone, and Internet device (PDA) used by many Wall Street analysts and professionals like me.

Bloomberg Television   A cable channel that broadcasts stock market and investment programming all day long.

Bonds   A debt investment security usually issued by a corporation or government (normally a long-term borrowing tool), promising to repay the principal upon maturity and paying stated interest at regular intervals.

Brokerage firm   A Wall Street investment banking firm dealing in stocks, bonds, and other financial investments, acting as both principal and agent, usually catering to institutions and individuals, providing investment banking services and securities trading and transactions.

Bubble Era   See '90s Bubble Era.

Bubble years   See '90s Bubble Era.

Bull market   A period of rising stock prices of more than 20% over at least a one-year timeframe. Widespread investor optimism. The 1990s represented one of the most notable bull markets in history.

Buyside   Institutions, such as mutual funds, hedge funds, pension funds, endowment funds, banks, insurance companies, and other major organizations, that do substantial investing. They "buy" stocks from and utilize Wall Street brokerage firms.

Buyside analyst Securities analysts employed by institutional investors to cover stocks internally that the firm owns or may be interested in buying. In-house portfolio managers are the audience and users of this internal research.

Call option (call) An investment instrument, a contract giving the owner a right to purchase usually 100 shares of the attendant stock at a fixed (strike) price until a specific (expiration) date. A speculation that the related stock price will rise. It allows participation in the stock price move of a large number of shares for a modest outlay. Can be highly volatile.

Capital gain The profit that results from the appreciation of a capital asset over its purchase price.

Capital gains tax The U.S. federal tax rate on profits or appreciation upon the sale of a stock or an investment holding, currently 15% if the position is held at least one year or the normal (higher) personal income tax rate if less than one year.

Capital spending The corporate expenditures on property, plant, and equipment. Not recorded as an immediate, upfront expense, but rather depreciated over a period of usually 5–20 years—the depreciation expense incurred on an ongoing basis.

Capitalized software Corporate computer software that, although purchased, is not accounted for as an upfront cost, but instead is depreciated over a period of years, enhancing current profitability.

Cash flow Corporate after-tax profits, plus other non-cash expenses such as depreciation/amortization. The inflow of cash to a company minus real, immediate, out-of-pocket expenses. The cash received and spent by a business during a fixed timeframe. An ultimate measure of a company's performance.

Cash flow statement One of the three principal financial statements required of all public companies, detailing the numbers that determine cash flow.

Cash generation See cash flow.

CEO A company's chief executive officer.

CFO A company's chief financial officer.

Chairman A company's head of the board of directors, the most senior position, above that of CEO or president.

Chart   See stock chart.

Chartered Financial Analyst (CFA)   The professional designation for financial analysts by the CFA Institute. Requires four years working experience in the investment business and the successful completion of three extensive examinations over a period of years. Indicates a high degree of professional qualification and standards.

CNBC   Cable channel owned by NBC, devoted almost exclusively to the stock market and investment content; programming runs all day long.

Commercial bank   The major banks used by a company for its corporate banking requirements (such as line of credit and short-term borrowing).

Commission   The fee charged by investment bank brokerage firm for buying and selling securities on behalf of its clients. The transaction charge to a major institution to trade a sizeable block of stock can be as little as a few pennies per share.

Compliance (legal)   Attorneys and other legal personnel at a brokerage firm that insure the firm adheres to securities laws and regulations. Involved in overseeing security analysts' research.

Computer services   The industry sector I covered as an analyst. Comprised of companies providing data processing services to corporate clients, such as payroll processing, datacenter outsourcing, credit card processing, and consulting.

Conference call   Normally, this refers to a broadcast and Q&A session by a company via telephone and/or webcast to Wall Street analysts and institutional investors. Conducted quarterly or at other intervals to discuss earnings results or to detail material news. Open to the public on a listen-in only basis.

COO   A company's chief operating officer, usually ranks below CEO but above CFO.

Correction   Euphemistic, misleading term commonly used to describe a stock market decline of less than 10%. The Street abhors negative references, preferring expressions that put a favorable face on gloomy investment elements.

Dead cat bounce   Even a dead cat, if it falls far enough, fast enough, will bounce upon hitting the ground. This refers to a stock that descends precipitously in price and then experiences a modest rebound. Don't think of the bounce as the beginning of a prolonged recovery.

Debt   Short- or long-term borrowings by a company, from drawn-down bank lines to long maturity bonds. Payment of short-term debt is due in less than one year, long-term debt beyond a year.

Debt-to-capitalization ratio   A company's long-term debt as measured against the total of long-term debt and stockholder's equity. Indicates the extent of debt leverage on the balance sheet—less than 20% is modest, and over 50% may be too high.

Deferred revenue   A company's sales that, for accounting purposes, are deferred into a future period and recorded later, diminishing immediate sales but enhancing future revenue.

Depreciation/amortization   Depreciation is the allocation of the cost of property, plant, and equipment over a period of years while the asset is being used to generate revenue. Amortization is the same, but pertains mainly to intangible assets such as goodwill, copyrights, patents, and trademarks.

Divestiture   Sale or disposition by a company of a business segment or division.

Dividend   Cash or stock paid by a company to its shareholders; normally an established amount consistent each quarter. Any revision is usually done annually.

Dividend payout ratio   The percentage portion of a company's net income paid out to shareholders in the form of dividends.

Dividend yield   The annual dividend amount per share as a percent of the current stock price.

Dow Jones Industrial Average (DJIA)   The most commonly used U.S. stock market index, comprised of thirty large capital companies, widely held stocks, price-weighted, the components occasionally removed and replaced to keep the index representative. Some of the current stocks in the index are 3M, American Express, ExxonMobil, Intel, Merck, Procter & Gamble, McDonald's, and Wal-Mart.

Earnings estimates   Security analyst forecasts of a company's earnings per share (EPS), usually for the current and next year, and each quarter of the current year. Published in virtually every research report and widely available over the Internet.

Earnings guidance   Corporate management forecast or direction pertaining to the expected results for the current and sometimes following year. Often disclosed publicly on conference calls or in earnings report press releases.

Earnings model/spreadsheet   An extensive, detailed, computer-generated company income statement as expected by a security analyst, usually for the current year and the following year, on a quarterly basis. Specifies assumptions on each line item (such as revenue, expenses, taxes, and share count) to derive earnings per share (EPS) estimate. Published in most research reports.

Earnings per share (EPS)   A company's net income divided by total shares outstanding, reported, or forecast on an annual and quarterly basis.

Earnings reports   Statements released each quarter by publicly held companies disclosing financial results for that period. Usually accompanied by commentary, spin, and a lot of rationalizing.

eBusiness   Internet-related businesses, sometimes referred to as eCommerce; a sexy term bantered widely during the '90 Bubble Era to hype stocks.

Economist   Experts employed by brokerage firms and banks to forecast future trends in the economy that may have an impact on the stock market [such as employment, GDP growth, interest rates, and the Consumer Price Index (CPI)—inflation]. Their influence on Wall Street has steadily diminished.

Emerging market stocks   Stocks in companies from rapidly developing countries or newly industrializing regions of the world, such as China, India, Brazil, and Southeast Asia.

Emphasis/recommended list   A brokerage firm's list highlighting its best stock ideas, and touting the strongest Buy opinions.

Equity   Stock or shares representing ownership in a company.

Exchange traded fund (ETF) Open-ended mutual fund, continuously traded in the market throughout the day (like a stock), precisely tracking various stock market indexes, sectors, stock groupings, or commodities. Low costs, actively traded.

Ex-dividend (date) A stock trades on this basis, that is, excluding the declared dividend, four days prior to "stock of record date" that determines which holders are entitled to the dividend. The price opens that day lowered in price by the amount of the dividend. Be aware of this date when selling a stock.

FASB (Financial Accounting Standards Board) A private, non-for-profit organization, originally stemming from the American Institute of Certified Public Accountants, with primary responsibility for establishing generally accepted accounting principles (GAAP) in the U.S. The SEC has designated the FASB to set accounting standards for publicly held U.S. companies.

Financial Analyst Journal The magazine published by the CFA Institute that features detailed academic studies and analyses on investment topics.

Financial consultant See retail broker.

Financial reengineering/restructuring Extensive balance sheet revamping; financial alterations. Activities, such as paying down debt, divestitures, stock repurchasing, and off-balance sheet financing, that often have the effect of enhancing earnings results.

Financials A company's income, balance sheet, cash flow statement, and other accounting statements.

Fortune 100 The top 100 U.S. corporations, ranked by gross revenues, as listed in the well-known Fortune 500 annual ranking.

GAAP (Generally Accepted Accounting Principles) earnings Earnings results reported by publicly held companies conforming to the accounting standards established by FASB. These are strict, conservative principles. It is common for companies to also present enhanced results by excluding certain expenses that are not FASB compliant, termed as "normalized" or pro forma.

GDP (Gross Domestic Product) Measurement of the size of a country's economy; market value of goods and services produced by a country in a specific timeframe (normally a year).

Growth stock   The stock of a company that is expanding rapidly, whose stock price should climb in sync with the company's progress. The cash it earns is reinvested in the firm's internal development. Little or no dividends are paid out.

Hard dollar fees   Payment to a brokerage firm for various services in actual dollars, rather than through commissions (soft dollars) from stock trades.

Hedge fund   Private investment funds such as DE Shaw, Bridgewater Associates, and Farallon Capital that are available to select, qualified high-income individual investors and institutions. They normally charge a 1%–2% fee and keep 20% of annual gains. Losses must be recovered before the 20% take out re-starts. They are largely exempt from regulation by the SEC and other bodies. Highly flexible investing strategies: short sales, futures, swaps, derivatives, almost any type of investing activity.

I. I. All-American team rankings   The annual ranking by *Institutional Investor* magazine of leading Wall Street brokerage firm security analysts, broken down by industry sectors, based on polling of buyside institutional investors.

Income statement   A company's profit and loss statement, reported quarterly, containing revenue (sales), various expenses, taxes, net profits (income), shares outstanding, and earnings per share. Indicates a company's operating progress. Foremost financial statement influencing the stock price.

Income-producing investment   An investment that returns a regular cash payment to the holder, such as a dividend paying stock or interest-bearing bond.

Index fund   A mutual fund that tracks a specific stock market or other financial market index such as the S&P 500, Dow Jones Industrial Average, and Wilshire 5000. Carries low fees.

Individual investor   A person performing his or her own investing; overseeing a personal portfolio; not acting on behalf of an investment institution.

Initial public offering (IPO)   A company's first sale of its shares to outside investors, to be traded in the stock market. Usually raises capital for corporate use (primary), sometimes insiders selling shares (secondary). Provides liquidity for previous holders; the shares can be bought and sold in the open market.

Institution   See institutional investor.

Institutional investor   An organization such as a bank, mutual fund, hedge fund, pension fund, insurance company, foundation, or money management firm that makes sizeable stock market investment transactions.

Institutional Investor (I.I.) magazine   The sophisticated, expensive, monthly publication aimed at Wall Street institutional investors, widely read by Street professionals, featuring investment-related topics such as research, money management, mutual funds, brokerage firms, investment banking, and leading personalities.

Institutional sales force/desk   A brokerage firm's sales personnel responsible for major institutional investor clients: transmits research information, takes orders to buy and sell stocks, assists in major trades, helps sell offerings and investment banking deals. Office location where these salespersons are clustered, often referred to as "sales desk."

Interest income   A fixed, guaranteed fee paid to holder of bond or other fixed income security; compensation to lender, paid out at specific intervals, usually every six months. The percentage of principal that fee represents is the interest rate.

Investment bank   A brokerage firm that assists companies and governments in issuing and selling securities to raise capital; offers merger and acquisition advice and makes markets in and trades stocks, bonds, commodities, and other instruments. Federal law was altered in 1999, enabling these firms to provide many commercial banking services.

Investment banker   A professional who works in the investment banking department of a Wall Street brokerage firm. Typically has corporate finance or public agency expertise. Assists organizations in raising capital/issuing securities, and merger/acquisition activities.

Investment banking   Services provided by a department of a Wall Street brokerage firm, pertaining to raising capital, strategic merger and acquisition consulting, and corporate finance. See investment bank, investment banker.

Investment opinion/rating   A brokerage firm security analyst's recommendation on a stock, such as Buy, Hold, or Sell.

Investment research committee   Various research management members, often including the market strategist, technician, legal compliance, and Director of Research, who review and sanction analyst opinion changes.

Investment risk   The possibility of permanent loss of capital. Prospect of losing money in an investment.

Investor relations (IR)   The department at a company that is responsible for contact with institutional investors, brokerage analysts, and individual investors. Provides information on the company that is of interest to investors, such as current business progress, order rate bookings, profitability, growth, and financial trends.

January effect   A stock market indicator; the direction of stock market during month of January, usually an accurate forecast of the trend for entire year.

Limit order   Order to buy or sell stock at a specific price, effective for the day or good until cancelled (compared to placing an order at the prevailing "market" price).

Lock-up period   The timeframe following an initial public offering when management, employees, and insiders are forbidden from selling their shares in the open market. Specified in the offering prospectus, usually a six-month span.

Long-term   The general Wall Street consensus of an investment holding period of more than one year. In my view, this timeframe should be at least two or three years. Federal capital gains tax of just 15% for securities held one year or more.

Margin (account)   A brokerage account allowing the client to borrow from the broker up to 50% of the value of the securities held in the account. Can be drawn down to purchase more stocks or for personal use.

Market strategist   An expert usually employed by brokerage firms to provide research and commentary on the overall stock market trends and direction, offering insightful investing observations and big-picture orientation.

Marketing   A security analyst function of communicating research via telephone and direct one-on-one meetings. Travel to different cities to meet with institutional clients is termed "marketing."

Model   See earnings model.

Morning call   The daily brokerage firm conference call over an internal squawk box system, usually around 7 or 8 AM Eastern time. Security analysts and other research professionals present their opinions, observations, and findings to the sales force, traders, and retail brokers.

Mutual fund   An investment pool with specific standards, goals, and strategies. Available to public investors; investment decisions made by a portfolio manager; value calculated at the end of each day (net asset value per share). Different types are growth, dividend yield, big cap, small cap, or industry sector focused. Offered by companies such as Fidelity, Vanguard, and American Funds.

NASD   National Association of Securities Dealers, a securities industry organization responsible for the self-regulation of the trading of stocks, corporate bonds, futures and options, and the activities of more than 5,000 brokerage firms.

NASDAQ   The name derived from National Association of Securities Dealers Automated Quotation system. The largest U.S. electronic screen-based equity securities market, encompassing some 3,200 stocks formerly known as over-the-counter (OTC) stocks, which are not listed on the NYSE or American Exchange.

Net income   A company's earnings after subtracting all costs and expenses (including taxes) from revenue. Sometimes referred to as the bottom line because it is at or near the end of the income statement. Earnings per share is net income divided by shares outstanding.

New York Stock Exchange (NYSE)   The largest listed stock exchange in the world, with more than 2,700 actively traded securities. These are mainly bigger capitalization stocks and more established companies than those traded on NASDAQ. NYSE stocks are generally more conservative investments than NASDAQ securities due to high listing standards.

Nikkei index   Nikkei 225 is the main stock market index in Japan; the Tokyo stock exchange, price-weighted, similar to the Dow Jones Industrial Average and/or S&P 500 in the U.S.

Off-balance sheet financing   Debt or asset financing that is not indicated on the balance sheet. Often pertains to activities such as leases, loan commitments, derivatives, letters of credit, and sometimes subsidiary liabilities.

Operating cash flow   The cash provided from a company's business operations before depreciation and amortization, excluding financing expenses such as interest and taxes.

Operating income   A company's income before depreciation and amortization, interest, and taxes.

Operating profit margin   A profitability measure of a company's basic business operations: operating income divided by revenue—that is, operating income as a percentage of revenue.

Organic growth   A company's internally generated revenue expansion, from the sale of goods and services, as opposed to acquisitions.

Outsourcing   An element of the computer services industry I covered as an analyst on Wall Street. The business of running an organization's computer datacenter, back office processing, and other data-processing activities, by an outside services firm.

PE multiple   Price-to-earnings ratio: the price of a stock divided by current or next year estimated earnings per share. Putting every stock on a similar basis allows value-price comparisons. The higher the PE, the more expensive the stock. Available in virtually every research report.

Pension fund   Retirement funds such as state and municipal employee pension plans that are major institutional investors with sizeable stock holdings.

Portfolio manager   The professional at a mutual fund, hedge fund, pension fund, etc., responsible for management of an institutional investment portfolio or other sizeable investment assets. Duties involve stock selection, asset allocation, financial analysis, investment monitoring, and other investment management functions.

Preferred stock   A class of stock senior to common stock, with superior rights in bankruptcy liquidation. Dividend is fixed over its life; no voting power; some similar characteristics to bonds.

Pre-tax profit margin   A company's income before taxes as a percentage of revenue—that is, income before tax divided by revenue. A common measure of profitability amongst companies.

Primary offering (issuance)   An issuance of shares by a company to raise capital, as opposed to a secondary offering. Can be an IPO or a follow-on offering.

Private client   See individual investor.

Private equity   An investment fund open only to select high income individuals and institutional investors; high initial investment requirement, normally above $100,000; limited partnership interests; invests in private companies, often purchasing publicly held firms— taking them private. The eventual gains on privately held companies via an IPO or sale to another company. Some leading firms are Blackstone, KKR, and Texas Pacific Group.

Pro forma earnings   A company's GAAP income adjusted to exclude non-recurring and extraordinary expenses such as restructuring costs and investment losses. Companies egregiously overuse this practice to sweeten the reported profit picture.

Profit   See net income.

Proxy statement   A company's annual disclosure to shareholders pertaining to voting in the election of the board of directors. Includes background information on board members and management, executive and board compensation, and identifies shareholders owning more than 5% of the stock.

Publicly held stocks   A company's shares that have been issued to the public, usually via an IPO, and are freely traded in the open market.

Put option (put)   An investment instrument; a contract giving the owner a right to sell usually 100 shares of the attendant stock at a fixed (strike) price until a specific expiration date. A speculation that the related stock price will decline. Allows participation in the stock price move of a large number of shares for a modest outlay. Can be highly volatile.

Recurring revenue   Continuous, predictable sales by a company generated from ongoing clients each quarter, year after year, from assured repeat business or long-term contracts. A highly visible revenue stream.

Reg FD (Regulation Fair Disclosure)   An SEC mandate that publicly traded companies disclose to all investors simultaneously, material information that might impact the stock. Eliminates some of the past selective disclosure to certain privileged institutional investors and security analysts, but has inhibited executive communication with investors.

REIT (Real Estate Investment Trust)   Company that invests in real estate; must distribute at least 90% of net income to shareholders and thus pays no corporate income tax. Shareholder pays normal income tax rate on dividends. The investment structure is similar to mutual funds.

Restriction period   The SEC required 40-day quiet period following an IPO during which the underwriting firm and insiders are prohibited from disclosing any information about the company that was not revealed in the prospectus. Security analyst at the underwriting firm cannot initiate research coverage on the stock during this span.

Retail broker   Sometimes has the title of financial consultant or financial advisor. The salesperson at a brokerage firm who focuses on individual investors (private clients, retail clients). Individual investor clients' main conduit to a brokerage firm's stock research.

Retail investor/client   See individual investor.

Retail producer   See retail broker.

Return on equity (ROE)   A company's annual net income as a percentage of the average level of stockholder's equity during the year. An important measure of return on stockholder's ownership interest—that is, a company's ability to generate earnings from net assets. Widely available in research reports.

Revenue   The funds a company obtains from sales of products/services in a specific period, disclosed quarterly and annually in the income statement. Sometimes termed "top line" (of income statement), often broken out by regions, products, or operating groups.

Revenue recognition   A method of recording revenue. The main accounting treatment is accrual basis: revenue recorded when service is performed or product is sold, even though payment may be in the future. Becomes more unclear with long-term contracts (percentage-of-completion accounting), deferred revenue, and installment sales.

Road show   Meetings with prospective institutional investors on a multi-city tour set up by an underwriting firm for corporate executives to pitch their story and entice participation in an offering. A similar outing is sometimes conducted, with no attendant offering, to boost the stock price (non-deal road show).

Royalty trust   Similar to REIT, usually in oil and gas or mining; pays no corporate taxes but is required to distribute at least 90% of its profits in the form of dividends. Investors pay personal income tax on dividends. Offers high dividend yields.

S&P 500   Standard & Poor's widely published broad stock market index that contains 500 large cap stocks. Several index funds and exchange traded funds track this index and are vehicles for investors to participate in the broad market.

Sales desk   See institutional sales force/desk.

SEC (Securities Exchange Commission)   Federal agency responsible for enforcing U.S. securities laws and regulating the securities industry and stock markets. Enforces public company disclosure standards and requirements to submit quarterly and annual 10-Q and 10-K reports.

Secondary offering (issuance)   The sale of management and insider stock to the public, endorsed by the company, sometimes part of an IPO, usually comes later.

Securities   The term referring to investment instruments in general, such as stocks, options, mutual funds, and bonds.

Security analysis   Research on companies and industries in order to determine the best, most appropriate stock investments. Evaluation and assessment of stocks to form investment recommendations such as Buy, Hold, and Sell.

Security analyst (investment analyst)   A professional at an investment bank brokerage firm, or on the buyside at an institutional investment firm, who conducts research on companies and industries in order to determine the best, most appropriate stock investments.

Selection committee   The brokerage investment bank's professionals who decide which stocks will be placed on its emphasis/recommended list, highlighting its best investment ideas. Usually comprised of Director of Research, market strategist, technical analyst, and other such members of research.

Sellside   The investment banks and brokerage firms that "sell" investment securities to institutions and individuals. They act as agents in trading securities, and sometimes as principal, when trading for their own account.

Shareholder   The owner of company's stock. Shares can be held in the Street name at a brokerage firm or retained directly in owner's name in certificate form.

Short position/sale   The trading tactic that bets on a decline in a stock price. Stock shares are borrowed from a brokerage firm and sold, with the requirement to repurchase and return them later, presumably at a lower price, generating a profitable trade. The short seller must pay the stock dividend to the brokerage firm so it can pass it on to the owner whose shares have been borrowed.

Short-term/near-term   The general Wall Street consensus of an investment or trading holding period of less than one year. The federal capital gains tax on securities held for under one year is a normal personal income tax rate.

Small cap stock   A company whose total outstanding shares have a value or market capitalization of under $5 billion. Sometimes small cap is defined as a $250 million to $1 billion valuation. Micro-cap is under $250 million, and mid-cap is $1 billion to $10 billion.

Squawk box   The brokerage firm's intercom broadcast system linking personnel, desks, and offices throughout the organization. Used often throughout the day to inform employees on business matters.

Stock appreciation rights (SARs)   A seldom-used corporate executive and employee incentive compensation plan that provides a cash bonus payment based on the rise in stock price on a specific number of shares during a stated period (usually one year).

Stock buyback/repurchase   An action by a company to purchase its own outstanding shares usually in the open market. The shares bought back are normally retired or retained in treasury for reissuing. The practice has risen dramatically in recent years. It is a temporary financial tactic to boost earnings per share and aid stock price.

Stock chart   A chart depicting company or market stock price trends and patterns, and trading volume, over specific time periods.

Stock options, employee   A widely-used corporate employee compensation incentive program giving the holder the right to purchase a specific number of the company's shares at a pre-set exercise price (normally the market price the day it was granted). Usually there is a vesting period of one or a few years before employee can exercise. Recent scandals involved illegal management backdating of the grant date at lower stock price, providing an immediate gain.

Stock recommendation   See investment opinion/rating.

Stock split   When a company expands the number of shares in the float, while at the same time reducing the price on an equivalent basis, to enhance liquidity. A 2-for-1 split doubles the number of shares and cuts the price in half. There is no benefit to the holder though the shares usually react positively to the news because it underscores that the company is experiencing robust performance and is often accompanied by a boost in the dividend.

Stop loss order   Investor order with a brokerage firm to buy or sell a specific security when a stated price is reached. Often used to protect a gain achieved in a stock by limiting the downside. In this case, once the limit price is hit, it triggers a market order to sell the shares.

Street, the   See Wall Street.

Tax rate   The corporate income taxes paid, specified on the income statement. Ranges as high as 39%. An expense deducted from revenues in determining net income. Derived by dividing tax expense by income before taxes.

Technical analysis   The use of charts in the study of stock and market price trends to predict future price direction. Presumes an efficient market that discounts all known factors in stock/market price. No consideration of fundamentals or business. Merits are controversial.

Technician/technical chartist   A Wall Street professional who performs technical analysis to formulate conclusions on future price movement.

Trader   The Wall Street brokerage firm or institutional investment professional who executes large-sized stock transactions, and who buys and sells securities on an extremely short-term basis (sometimes only seconds or minutes) to exploit small price changes and generate gains for the in-house account.

Trading desk   Location in a brokerage or institutional investor firm where traders are clustered. A noisy, chaotic, wild scene of intense activity and high-pressure dealings.

Treasurys   U.S. government debt to finance deficits: treasury bills (T-bills) have a maturity of under one-year; notes, from one to ten years; and bonds, more than 10 years. Guaranteed interest rate; the lowest risk investment. Current interest rate on widely traded 10-year. Treasury note is the most common indicator of interest rate direction in the economy.

Turnaround   A company's efforts, following negative setbacks and disappointing performance, to reverse the course and reconfigure the business to reestablish a positive earnings trend. Usually encompasses new management, lay-offs, divestitures, financial restructuring, and PR hoopla.

Unbilled revenue   A company accounting policy that records earned revenue that, under contract terms, the customer cannot yet be billed. A liberal accounting technique, broken out on the balance sheet.

Underwriting   An investment bank brokerage firm's action of undertaking the risk of issuing (selling) stock or bonds on behalf of a company or government. Once a price has been agreed to at the time of issuance, the investment banking syndicate guarantees the proceeds to the issuer.

Value stock   Shares that appear to be trading at a discount relative to other stocks—under priced or inexpensive based on fundamental analysis. Often carry a low PE multiple or price-to-book value ratio, and/or high dividend yield. Sometimes defined as stock selling below intrinsic value or at a "sensible" price.

Venture capital (VC)   A limited partnership fund that invests in high-risk start-up companies. Because of the speculative nature, the start-up is unable to borrow major sums from banks or obtain equity financing from the public with an IPO. A VC fund obtains a sizeable equity position with a goal of gaining a big return on invested capital.

Volatility   A specious term often used to describe a declining stock market. Rarely utilized in characterizing a rising market.

Wall Street (The Street) Refers to the broad securities business; sometimes a more narrow term depicting New York-based investing banking and brokerage firms.

Webcast A broadcast by executives over the Internet of a company's quarterly results; commentary and Q&A with Street institutional investors, security analysts, and the public.

Wire house A brokerage firm predominantly focused on retail, individual investor clients; not serving big institutional investors or providing investment banking services.

Write-off An accounting action reducing the value of an asset or investment on a company's balance sheet (taking a loss) because the expected return has diminished or vanished.

INDEX